KILLING

AMERICA

The Death of Our Republic

THOMAS A. MOORE

Second Printing: Killing America, The Death of our Republic

Author: Thomas A. Moore

Copyright 2018

Design, Interior Formatting, Editing and Research: Liz Moye Moore

All Scripture, unless otherwise noted comes from the Living Bible Paraphrase and the King James Versions of the Holy Bible

Also available in eBook form

ISBN - 13:978-1987546651
ISBN – 10:1987546652

Acknowledgements

This book is dedicated to my grandfather, William A. Taylor who left this earth nearly three decades ago. I truly miss our conversations about theology, history, philosophy and politics. You left a definitive print on my heart and life for which I am eternally grateful.

I wish to express my gratitude to my wife Liz, whose excellence and professionalism in editing, formatting and publishing my books are a significant contribution in the time-consuming completion of all my writings.

It is always my desire to honor Jesus in all that I write. To God be the glory!

Table of Contents

Introduction

Many years ago, I stumbled upon a few books which opened my eyes to some information that on the surface stirred my curiosity but didn't at first compel me to dive into a full investigation. I had always been an openminded, but logical truth seeker; so I ignored the persistent temptation to dismiss this new information as "conspiracy theories" and eventually plunged ahead with my new discoveries. There were simply just too many connected dots for a full dismissal. At that time, the newly discovered and publicly physical documented evidence demanded of me a private and conclusive mental verdict that would not allow me the option of ceasing my investigations. I pressed on!

Prior to my discoveries, I had always surmised that I lived in a free country with free and fair elections, and with fully secured individual rights and liberties. I had a limited, yet vague understanding of our Constitution and our Republic form of government. But I had no working knowledge of the 64 families who owned much of the world's wealth and who were referred to as "the Globalists, the Elites, the One-worlders, and the Cabal," whose primary goal was to destroy or at least diminish the independent sovereignty of every industrial nation so they could fully implement their "New World Order."

The deviant designed plan for the destruction of our nation has worked so brilliantly and efficiently that many now believe it could not have been accomplished by mere human means. Some have even speculated and suggested that perhaps a "supernatural force" or "higher power" has orchestrated the whole thing.

This book is a brief and introductory culmination of my findings, interwoven with biblical prophecies that many centuries ago predicted this sinister and all-encompassing end-time global government.

Prologue

He called me over to his bedside and asked me to lean my ear close to his face, so he could whisper something of vital importance. My grandfather was approaching the day that marked his ninety-second year since he arrived on this earth, and he was simultaneously rapidly approaching the day of his departure. I was somewhat elated to hear what this man had to say to me. What would be the dying words of this one who had worked hard all his life to provide for his family; this man who as a construction foreman had built many of the campus buildings at Marshall University in Huntington, West Virginia, as well as supervised the construction of the secret underground sanctuary at the Greenbrier Resort that was built for the protection of the President of the United States in the unlikely event of an emergency? What wonderful words of wisdom would come out of the mouth of this man who for the entirety of his life had read the Bible completely through many times and had rarely missed a Sunday morning church service or the opportunity to invest financially in the Kingdom of God by faithfully submitting his tithes and offerings? What profundity would exude from this one who had lived through four major wars, the "Great Depression," many Presidential administrations and a myriad of diverse cultural changes? With much anticipation, I leaned forward to hear what

I was expecting to be life-changing words of wisdom directly from the Almighty through the lips of my dying grandpa.

Here's what he spoke to me in his weak, yet resolute voice:

"First, Thomas, promise me you will never buy a foreign car, especially one made by the Japanese! Second-- promise me you will never, NEVER vote for a damned Democrat!"

With these two requests, he dozed off into a long nap before I felt compelled to respond with a verbal promise I might not be able to keep. I couldn't resist the temptation to emit a quiet chuckle under my breath, in response to his uncharacteristic usage of the word "damned." It just struck me as funny for some strange reason. His first request was a bit troublesome for me, for in my seventeen-year history of experiences with cars, I discovered time and time again that the foreign made cars of the seventies and eighties were so much more durable, dependable and mechanically sound than the American ones I had owned (not to mention, more fuel efficient). But I completely understood his request to not invest in the economies of foreign countries who at one time were our sworn enemies and had killed thousands of our sons in times of war-- including my grandfather's son who was killed when the Japanese bombed his platoon. My uncle John Taylor was a chaplain in WWII when he lost his life serving his country. My grandpa, William Alden Taylor was naturally devastated when he got the news of losing his only son. And because he was a hard-working, blue collar, tax-paying, church going, God fearing Republican, his last request was for me to promise that I would never vote a left-leaning Democrat into a political office; nor purchase a car from those "Japs" who had mercilessly murdered his sweet, kind, Christ-loving son.

My grandpa didn't know much about my political views at this juncture. We mostly discussed theology (my major in college) and it was assumed by him that I had inherited my parents' conservative political views. I was at the ripe "old" age of thirty-three during this time, and I had witnessed the beginnings of the Democratic Party undergoing several significant paradigm changes in the decade of the eighties! I had always made it a point to vote for the man... not for the Party! And my vote was cast for the person whose philosophies and ideologies best represented the Bible. The Word of God has always been my standard and authority pertaining to which political candidate I would choose to support. As far as political, social, moral, and economic issues were concerned-- what mattered to God, mattered to me. What He deemed to be of utmost importance concerning political issues was my only focus and concern.

Even though I fulfilled my duty by voting in most elections on the state and federal level, I considered myself to be a novice or even apolitical throughout the decade of my twenties. I was far from being viewed as one who was politically astute! It wasn't until I taught World History, US History, US Government and Economics, Apologetics and Logic on the high school level that my interest in the political arena began to emerge and escalate. I also discovered that my great, great, great uncle was a signer of the Declaration of Independence (Button Gwinnett), and his nephew (my great, great grandfather- David Gwinnett) had fought in the War for Independence to secure the many freedoms I was enjoying at this time in my life (I recently visited the grave of David near Monterey, Va.).

I wondered why my grandpa thought it to be so vastly and vitally important to give his last instructions to me in the way of politics. After all, there were several leaders at that time in the Democratic Party on the national and state levels who claimed to love Jesus and seemed to be sincerely concerned for the rights of the poor, the homeless, the starving, the uneducated, the outcasts, the minorities-- the very kinds of people about whom Jesus was concerned and the very ones He commanded us to minister to. In the decades of the fifties, sixties, seventies and early eighties, it seemed to me that the Democrats were always fighting for those "under-dog" constituents who could not fight for themselves. They were the Party who seemed to demonstrate the most love, mercy, and compassion toward the underprivileged. Or at least, that's how it appeared to me. Even though I never supported anyone in this Party, I would have never, back in those days, referred to them as those "damned Democrats!" Maybe slightly deceived. Maybe a bit arrogant. Maybe misled. But not "damned!"

But in the eighties, I began to notice a deceptive, subtle, paradigm shift or slippery slope of the Party that continued to persistently claim to represent Jesus to the poor, yet stealthily introduced radical legislation that not only was incongruent with God's Word but was also antithetical to the philosophical principles of our founding fathers.

It became extremely obvious that there was an underlying, sinister agenda behind their deceptive mask of "compassion" that had an unmistakable glare and that catapulted my interest to dive into the controversial world of politics with the sincere purpose and goal of discovering first-hand how world events and political structures fit into the prophecies I had spent years investigating in the Scriptures.

As the decade of the eighties came to an end, it became very clear to me that those who claimed to follow Christ and at the same time represented and embraced the

Democratic Party were either ignorant of the Scriptures or politically challenged. They were either lacking in the knowledge of God's Word as they were being duped by the new religion of political correctness... or they knew exactly what they were doing in propagating their agenda to get the unsuspecting masses feeding from their trough of socialist liberalism! I wanted to design a bumper sticker for my newly purchased American made vehicle that said: "To be a follower of Christ and a liberal Democrat is an oxymoron!" The two philosophical differences are diametrically opposed to one another. They just don't jive in any possible manner!

My further research on the political evolution of the "Progressives" has led me to organize my thoughts and conclusions in this book. This is not by any means or stretch of the imagination an exhaustive book describing the historical documentation of our two-Party system. It is merely my attempt to expose the delusional dichotomy of those on the left who are convinced that their policies will usher in some form of utopian government that will benefit not only all Americans, but the entire global populace in a positive manner and on a grandiose scale. The absurdities of the ideals on the left are so strikingly evident, I cannot begin to comprehend how anyone can be so foolish to embrace them. In the natural realm, it just doesn't make any sense! But in the spiritual realm, it all becomes so unmistakably clear! And it is no longer just those "damned Democrats" who are "the blind leading the blind!" The repulsive Republicans have accepted the competitive challenge from the Left and have become exuberant participants in their sinister game of "Let's See Who Can Destroy America First!"

1

Religion and Politics

In my generation, we constantly heard these two idioms:

1.)   Religion and politics don't mix. We should keep them separate!

2.)   At social gatherings (holiday meals with the family), the subjects of religion and politics are taken off the table. They are forbidden! So don't discuss them!

For years I have observed men like Jerry Falwell Sr. being interviewed by the media for his response to key political issues in the forefront of the public. He was the "go to" conservative for wisdom on controversial issues of his day. He was constantly criticized by those on the "left" who ferociously attacked him with these words:

"Jerry should stay out of politics. He should just stay in his pulpit and preach about the love of God. He is a hate monger who stirs things up and causes more division in our nation. He should be unifying instead of dividing. He is a preacher... not a politician. He should shut up and stay out of the political arena!"

These same liberals had no issues or reservations whatsoever with the Reverend Jesse Jackson, Reverend Al Sharpton, Reverend Louis Farrakhan, and Reverend Jeremiah Wright who entered the political fray representing and furthering their socialistic policies. The "libs" held these men as champions of their cause to fundamentally change the role of our government on every social and economic issue in every segment of our society. These liberal "ministers of God" were held in the highest of esteem by those who opposed every sound and healthy political policy for the direction of our country. They could do no wrong. The involvement of these "reverends" in politics was welcomed, embraced, and even celebrated. But not Jerry's! As an American tax-paying citizen, Jerry had just as much a right to discuss and debate the hot political issues of his day as did his counterparts Jesse, Al, Jeremiah and Louis. But the libs didn't see it that way!

The Word of God is replete with a smorgasbord of every moral, economic, social and political issue that affected each generation in the history of mankind. The Bible is teeming with God's specific and non-negotiable instructions for His people in all matters pertaining to the philosophical and practical issues of judicial and governmental rule that would assist His people in pleasing Him and in living in peace and harmony with each other. One simply cannot separate religion from politics. The two are inseparable because God has ordained them both. One highly affects the other. Just as morality and righteousness cannot be legislated by human governments, neither can they be dismissed or ignored by the same! God is the Supreme Law Giver!

Conversing about the topics of religion and politics should never be avoided. Healthy debates about the character and nature of God, mixed with the policies of governmental rule have been perpetuated for centuries. King Solomon refers to these sessions in his record of maxims of wisdom (Proverbs) by calling the geographical place of hot debates on civic issues "the gate!" This is where men of God met every day to discuss current events.

This is where these folks let it all hang out with no reservations about how they felt or how they thought regarding the latest decree of the King. Did the political, theological and philosophical sparks fly? Absolutely! For Solomon records, "As iron sharpens iron, so does the countenance (opinions) of one man sharpen the other!" This wise King recognized the healthy benefits of vigorous civil debates.

When one studies the history of the world, one discovers that in every generation there was a place near town where healthy discussions took place. Men gathered to discuss the ideas and philosophies of Socrates, Plato, and Aristotle. In the first few centuries after Christ left the earth, Christians and Jews discussed their differences of opinion on Jesus-- Was He indeed the Messiah, or an impostor? Greeks and Romans debated on the best form of government to pursue. In the beginnings of our young nation, our religious forefathers gathered on a daily basis to entertain the notion that they could become a free and independent nation. The process whereby they would arrive at that mutual goal varied amongst them. The debates were heated! The sparks flew! Even though they were unwilling to compromise on their personal convictions, they prayed together, seeking the right answers from God concerning the mutual challenges and dilemmas they faced in perilous times. They knew God had a plan! They were convinced He had brought them safely over the ocean to establish a country where they would have the freedom to worship Him, unobtrusive from any tyrannical monarchy. Their mandate was clear in establishing a form of government that would honor God and that would be "of the people, by the people, and for the people." A government that served the people-- not the other way around. They also understood the wisdom and necessity of including God and His biblical instructions for the proliferation and continuation of a strong and healthy

government. And guess what? It worked--
for a very long time! Unfortunately, in the
present, the "God factor" has been
removed. And we are beginning to see the
consequential evidences of that arrogant
decision to disregard the instructions for
government given by the very One who
created us!

"Separation of Church and State" is the
excuse of the liberals for their removal of
anything and everything pertaining to God
from the public arena. Whether it be a
statue, a painting, a nativity scene, the
words "Merry Christmas," or the Ten
Commandments posted on the courthouse
building, the liberals have been successful
in removing any hint of an absolute, moral
value system against which we measure
what form of government and justice we
meet out. They have erroneously
concluded that "separation of church and
state" should include removing anything
that hints of the true God of the Scriptures
from the public square and from the

governmental systems on the city, county, state, and federal levels.

However, when one takes a look at the original premise and objective of the founding fathers who included this idea of the separation of church and state, it becomes obvious that they did not want a state-established church to dictate to them how and when to worship. Their horrific experiences with such a government sanctioned church in England propelled them to include this idea in their earliest writings. In other words, they specifically wanted to secure the rights of each American to worship where and how he/she desired, with no dictates from the newly formed government. It was clear they wanted the government out of the church-- not God out of the government! By their writings, we can unmistakably conclude that they never intended to remove God or religion from the government or from the education system or from the courthouse. On the contrary, they knew that without the involvement of Almighty God in every aspect of our lives, including the rule of civic law, they were doomed for failure with this new experiment of a "democratic/republic" form of government. They advocated freedom OF religion—not freedom FROM religion!

A quick glance at the rise and fall of governments in history will convince any honest thinking person that when God is removed from the public sector, confusion and deception ensue! When God's instructions on how to govern a nation are flippantly ignored, chaos and anarchy become the rule of the day. And in nearly every country, kingdom, or nation where the instructions of God have been mocked or ignored, out of the anarchy has arisen a tyrannical dictator who postured himself as the hero who convinced the desperate masses that he was exactly what they needed to lift them out of the mess of confusion, poverty and despair. These evil rulers deceptively convinced those "helpless victims" that if they would just trust him by obeying his every command and order, they would be lifted out of the political mess of anarchy and live peaceful and affluent lives.

These evil dictators continued their lies by stating that for the good of the nation, the people must first give up their guns so that order, peace, and safety can be restored. Then, they must give up their personal property so that everyone will be on equal ground. They must also give up their religion because after all, everyone knows that every war in the world was caused by fanatical religious zealots. History is replete with many examples of this progression of the destruction of once powerful nations who succumbed to the dictates of tyrants who controlled the masses through the incremental diminishing of individual rights and freedoms-- all accomplished under the guise of "public safety!"

Liberal Democrats today are on the same slippery slope path that is leading to the destruction of our once sovereign nation. They are either fools who are ignorant of world history, or they are intelligent creatures who know exactly what they are doing. Or, there is a third option: They are deceived pawns in the hands of higher powers who have a sinister plan to rule the world and need to destroy this nation in order to accomplish the fulfillment of their plans for global totalitarianism.

The socialist liberals of today believe that anything pertaining to biblical Christianity must be kept out of our public schools, out of our courts, and out of our entire government. But they have no problem whatsoever welcoming Muslims into our country and embracing their Sharia Laws and their religion of Islam. To the liberals, any religion is acceptable in the public sector except Christianity. To them, the Bible has no place in politics or in the education process of our children. But the

Koran, (which commands all Muslims to kill everyone who doesn't embrace their religion), is quite tolerable and even embraced.

If religion and politics don't mix, and there should be "separation of church and state," then why is Islam embraced in our schools and in our government?

Recently, I applied for a temporary teaching position for a History class in a large local High School. Since I had taught history fulltime for several years, the administrator invited me for an interview and basically told me that the job was mine. I excused myself during the interview to get some water, when I noticed a plaque hanging on the wall just outside this man's office. It read:

"This award is given to (name of school) in appreciation for your recognition and embracement of the Muslim religion and culture of Islam."

This High School had a policy that no Bibles would be allowed on their campus. The teachers could not say, "Merry Christmas" (they had to say "Happy Winter Holidays"). No mention of Jesus (even in a historical context) by the teachers was allowed. Any references to Christianity were forbidden. All in the name of "separation of church and state." Needless to say (but I'll say it anyway), I turned down the job offer! Thanks to the socialist liberals in our city, county, state, and federal governments, the name of God and the religion of Christianity have been squashed and deleted. But the religions of Marxism, Hinduism, New Age Universalism, Islam, Darwinism, and Secular Humanism continue to be embraced and taught in our public education institutions—because these religions fit into the agenda of the New World Order Globalists who want a one-world religion under their one-world government! In their minds, true Christianity is just too abrasive, divisive, and counterproductive for their global cause of "unity."

What ever happened to "freedom of religion" and "freedom of speech?" The Marxists socialists running our country have killed them! But God is not One to be ignored, disregarded, or "killed" without dire consequences! When the Globalists killed the biblical concept of the God of Truth in every sector of our government and society, they simultaneously killed America!

2

The Illusion of Freedom

Most American citizens would concur that we live in a free nation. We are under the illusion that we have the freedom to make our own decisions pertaining to education, religion, careers, and family. In these specific areas, we still have some measure of freedom to choose. But consider the following:

We can own property-- but in reality, it never truly belongs to us. When we purchase a home, we pay several taxes and legal fees up front at closing. We pay annual property taxes to the government even after we have paid off the bank loan. When we leave this earth and our child inherits the house and land, he/she must pay an inheritance tax and continue paying annual property taxes for many years. Are we really deceived to think that WE own that house and land? Try not paying your property taxes and see what happens. You will eventually be evicted from your own home and the government will seize your property. You don't own it! You never have, and you never will! And that's not freedom! That's property confiscation which leads to the slippery slope of tyranny! And the founding fathers warned us of this!

We live in the mountains of a state that was one of the original thirteen colonies of our Republic. Upon our arrival here, my neighbor related a horror story of an ongoing legal battle with the state government which had used their "eminent domain" laws to successfully steal 80 acres of his property from him. My friend showed me the documentations of ownership by his ancestors that go way back to the late 1700's. The courthouse records confirmed that his family had owned this large chunk of land for over two centuries. After he had paid thousands of dollars in legal fees and attorney fees, the court awarded the property to the state. To add insult to injury, the state never presented a just cause to the court for their confiscation of his legally owned land. There were no building plans for a water tower or a cell phone tower. No plans to construct a highway. No plans at all! Years later, we still have no clue why the state wanted that land at the very sharply pitched top of this mountain. In our estimation, the land serves no use whatsoever to them. But without reasonable cause, they stole it from our neighbor. Does this sound like we live in a free country to you? But there's more-- the "eminent domain" laws require that the state compensate landowners for the seizure of their personal property. The amount is at the discretion of the state government. Our friend had already paid property taxes in excess of approximately $75,000 to the state for the duration of his "ownership!" And this didn't even include the required property taxes and inheritance taxes paid to the state by his forebears over many years.

Consider the fact that everything we do is taxed by our own government (That's right, the very government that was created by our founding fathers that was supposed to serve us, not the other way around). If we want to hunt and fish, we must purchase a license. If we want to drive, we must buy a driver's license. If we want to "own" a car, we pay a sales tax, annual property tax, annual tag fee, annual registration fee, annual state inspection fee, and annual insurance fee (not to mention the gas tax each time we fill up our tanks). Every car we buy has a "chip" in it so that the government can track every move we make. Still think you are "free?" If we want to start our own business or build a house, we must first pay for a license or purchase a building permit. Whatever we purchase from a store, we pay sales taxes. We are taxed for everything... and we own nothing! Is that what "freedom" looks like?

Even our tax system is set up as a "control" mechanism by our government. Ours is a "progressive tax" system that has been devised to usher in a socialistic style of government through a sneaky redistribution of wealth. It punishes those who work hard building a successful business (that provides many more jobs for others) by taxing them at a higher rate; while it rewards those who invest little time, energy, and effort by taxing them less. This tax system is clearly a mask for socialism which historically in other countries has led to a dictatorial government of totalitarianism, i.e., people control.

The United States is the leading industrial nation with the highest corporate tax rate. Does that represent "freedom?" In most states, our children are told by the government which school they must attend (K-12). Doesn't sound like freedom to me. And if as parents you make the financial sacrifice to put your children in private schools, you are still required by the government to pay taxes that go toward the public schools of your neighborhood. You cannot opt out of the mandate to financially support your local government run schools. No freedom of choice there, my friend!

Little by little, piece by piece, slice by slice, the liberal socialists of our own government are incrementally eroding our individual liberties and freedoms to choose. The Elites who govern our nation and states think they know best how to run our lives, our families, our educational system, our healthcare and our businesses. If this continues, it won't be very long before they dictate where you can attend church... or IF you can attend church!

3

The Illusion of a Democratic-Republic

Our founding fathers created a representative, democratic-republic form of government with three branches of "checks and balances" in order to maintain balance and accountability and in order to give the common people a vote and a direct voice in what was supposed to be THEIR government. We have lost it!

Congress (the legislative branch) was created to represent each state in making laws that would protect the constituents of those states against an arrogant federal government with too much power. The courts (the judicial branch) were created to interpret those new laws and ascertain the constitutional validity of those laws. The office of the Presidency (the executive branch) was created to enforce those new laws.

For the past 80 years, the roles of these branches have become so blurred that one can no longer recognize their original intended function. The Supreme Court is making the laws by legislating from the bench. The President has the power of the pen to write "executive orders," essentially bypassing Congress and implementing laws "for the good of the American people!" The House of Representatives has lost all of its power and authority and has been reduced to a group of "figure heads" only. The Senate has been bought out by special interest groups, lobbyists, and socialist globalists, and pushes through legislation that benefits the foreigners who are putting millions of dollars into their pockets instead of benefiting the American citizens they were elected to represent.

Time and time again we observe the people of a state going to the polls to vote on a moral, social, or economic issue and overwhelmingly passing that specific agenda by as much as 70 percent of the votes. And time and time again we observe how a three-member court of liberal socialists over-rule the will of the majority in that state. That's right-- three people had the power to over-turn the will and the votes of millions of tax-paying citizens. This is not a "Democracy!" This is an "Oligarchy," which means the power to rule rests with a very small number of people who control every facet of the lives of the masses. This "rule of the few over the many" has destroyed any semblance of democracy in this nation. What this tells us is that our vote no longer matters, which means that our voice no longer matters, which means that we are fooling ourselves if we still think that we have a democratic republic form of government. It has been thoroughly and completely destroyed! Vanished!

The courts at every level were originally created to interpret the laws passed by Congress and signed by the President (or the Governor at the state level). They were not created to make laws. But they now have way too much power in squashing any law passed by Congress and signed by the President or voted on by the majority of citizens in each state. That's not democracy, my friend. That's not the representative form of government our founding fathers created. And that's not freedom!

As of the writing of this book, the most recent elections on the national and state levels were tainted by millions of illegal, non-citizens voting and by pre-rigged voting machines. The evidence is there, but nothing was done about it. In all of these cases, the liberal Democrats were behind these events to ensure that their candidates would win.

Many of my friends in the Charlotte, NC area went to the polls to vote for the conservative candidates. When they pulled the lever of the machines, all of the Democratic candidates popped up before their eyes with a check beside each of their names. Obviously, they reported this, but nothing was done about it. This happened all over the United States including here in my own state where the liberal Democratic Governor barely squeezed out a victory through voter fraud that included illegal immigrants voting, dead people voting, out-of-state citizens voting, and rigged voting machines. We are not talking about a few thousand illegal votes. We are talking about millions of fraudulent votes to secure the victory for the liberal candidates. (There has not been one documented incident of a Republican being involved with any election fraud. Just as there has not been one registered Republican that has been involved with any mass shootings or erratic behavior in destroying property or hurting people when rioting in the streets). The voice of the average American citizen is no longer heard by those arrogant Elitists in our government who no longer work for us but have sold out to the Globalists. The votes of hard-working, tax-paying American citizens don't count any more. Elections are rigged by a group of people who have duped us into thinking we still have a Democratic-Republic where our votes still matter. Let's find out who some of these people are, and the process by which they came to power.

4

The Massive Influence and Power of the Elitists

My investigations in my years of research have concluded that over 70 percent of the world's wealth is now in the hands of 64 families who control much of the world's corporations and natural resources. The old adage: "He who has the gold rules" is not to be taken lightly. These few powerful people own banks, corporations, governments, heads of states, and yes... even our very own Presidents, Senators, and Judges! With a nod of the head and a stroke of the pen, these Elitists can fund, influence, and instigate riots, bankruptcies, corporate mergers, national elections, and even wars. For years they have groomed, educated, and financed their hand-picked candidates in our elections on both sides of the political spectrum. Republicans and Democrats alike are in their political and financial pockets.

Those candidates postulating themselves as "Christian conservatives" and those portraying themselves as "progressive socialists" are being financially propped up and "fed" by these few wealthy families. And these puppet political candidates will never bite the hand of those puppeteers who feed them, nor will they ever cut the puppet strings that control their every move. Let's take a brief look at a few of the names of these families and the organizations and corporations which they fund, own, or control:

The Hearst family
The Rockefeller family
JP Morgan
The Rhodes family (Rhodes Scholars)
The Vanderbilts
The Duke family
The DuPont family (Free Masons and Trilateral Commission)
The Rothschilds
The Soros family
The Bundy family (Illuminati, CFR, CIA)
The Collins family
The Freeman family (The satanic New Age Movement)
The Kennedys
The Onassis family
The Reynolds family (Reynolds Tobacco, Free Masons)
The Carnegie Family
The Russell family (Jehovah's Witnesses, a front for Illuminati satanists)

The Templeton family
The Bilderbergs
Bill Gates
Queen Elizabeth and her family
The Bohemian Grove
The Illuminati
The Skull and Bones Secret Society
The Free Masons
Chase Manhattan and Citi Corp
The Bank of London
The United Nations
The European Union
The World Bank
The World Court
The World Council of Churches
The International Monetary Fund (IMF)
Bank of America
Wells Fargo Bank
Goldman Sachs
Standard Oil (renamed "Saudi Aramco")
Shell Oil
Sinopec Oil
China National Petroleum Corp
Exxon Mobile
The International Red Cross

The American Red Cross
FEMA
Planned Parenthood
Pharmaceutical Companies: Johnson and
Johnson, Roche, Pfizer, Novartis, Sanofi,
GlaxoSmithKline, Merck & Co., AbbVie,
Bayer, Abbot Labs, (the list goes on).
The Food and Drug Administration (FDA)
TV networks: ABC, NBC, CBS, ESPN, CNN,
FOX News, Public Television, C-Span,
Cable, Direct TV (the list goes on).

Now you might ask, "So what? Most of these corporations have helped a lot of people. They have even done much good to a great number of our American citizens!" And that is exactly the attitude and response that these wealthy families want you to have.

These Globalist trillionaires have deceptively put a palatable, benevolent, cosmetic face on each of these organizations and corporations so that the masses will think that they serve a good and noble purpose. For instance, the Free Masons have been funded by these families to assist them in their quest for people control and world dominance. The delightful (but deceptive) cosmetic face of the Masons is the construction by the "Shriners" of many hospitals for children who have been badly burned. They then fund the TV commercials that show sweet innocent children who are pleading for your financial assistance to help them get well. This is a facade to pull at our emotional heart strings to support their agenda of a "New World Order" which will, in effect, eventually eliminate the sovereign status of each independent nation by blending them into a One-world Government! The same is true for the Red Cross and FEMA organizations-- nothing but a cosmetic "front" or window dressing to hide a destructive, sinister plan for world dominance and control. Now, let's see how these Elite families have gained control over the United States of America and have successfully killed our Republic!

5

The Surreptitious Take Over

Not too many decades ago the Federal Reserve Act was conceived and birthed. With the stroke of a pen our once sovereign nation became a corporation. These 64 families invested in this newly formed corporation by essentially buying it out! They have for decades controlled how their puppets vote in Congress, who gets to run for President (on both sides), who is picked for the federal courts and state courts, and how they want us to vote. Under the guise of a "free democracy" they have fundamentally changed everything about how our government is run and how we get to live out our lives. They used our democratic system of government to come into power, and then destroyed that very system in just a few quick decades. The following are the means or "vehicles" through which they rapidly and deceptively gained total control of our American government and culture, and how they now have their hands in every societal nook, crack, and cranny of our everyday lives:

Water supply
Oil supply
Food supply
The Banks
Military (NATO)
The Internal Revenue Service (IRS)
Taxes (including social security)

Public Education (K through College)
Media (printed press and television)
Movie and music industries
Mind-altering drugs (prescription pharmaceuticals)
The Democratic Party
The Republican Party
The Council on Foreign Relations (CFR)
The Trilateral Commission
The Central Intelligence Agency (CIA)
The office of the President and the Courts
The Environmental Protection Agency (EPA)
Illegal Immigration (DACA)
Planned Parenthood
The American Civil Liberties Union (ACLU)
The NAACP
Gun Control (confiscation)
Social Services - Welfare
Unions (Teamsters, National Education Assoc.)
(And the list goes on)

Let's briefly discuss several of these conduits for manipulation and control:

It goes with saying (but I'll say it anyway) that water is the basic element without which we cannot survive. The Elitists have harnessed and gained control over virtually every original resource of water in most of the largest industrial nations, including our own. In some of our own states here in America, their puppets in our government have passed laws that forbid its own citizens from collecting rain water or digging a well or pond on their own land because of a convenient "recent" discovery of an ant or worm that is on the "endangered species list!" Why would they be more concerned about an ant than a human being? We'll get to that later! These few wealthy families own several bottled water companies, which have as many harmful ingredients in their water as the fluoride and chloride that they have instructed their political cronies in city governments to add to our water supply. They know that if they can control all the water, they can control all the people.

Oil has become the most treasured commodity of our modern world. Everything in our society is dependent on a vast, never-ending oil supply. If the oil is stopped, the society cannot function. We have no gas to drive to work! Cornering the market and gaining total control of the oil companies of the world was a must for these Globalist Elites. They know that if they control the oil-- they control the people. The Rockefellers led the way in solving this problem and attaining this goal. Through the Environmental Protection Agency (EPA) they successfully shut down nearly every oil field in Texas, Oklahoma, and Alaska; and abruptly halted all operations of off-shore drilling by our (their) government-- all under the deceptive guise of "cleaner air, water, and soil." The 64 family members effectively shut down our economy and forced us to be dependent on foreign oil. This was a huge step toward losing what little we had left of our independent sovereignty! This was no accidental fluke! This was by design!

Food: Several decades ago, the handpicked US Congressmen and women were instructed by these Elites to vote on shutting down the farmers who were supplying most of our food. To make it look good (cosmetic window-dressing), thousands of American farmers were financially subsidized by our tax dollars to actually cease from growing any more food. They were paid by our government (run by the Elites) to let their fertile soil remain fallow. Now, only a small percentage of "government owned" farmers (4 percent) are producing the food supply for over 300 million American citizens. This plan, like all the rest, was successful in gaining total control over our entire food supply. Control the food-- control the people! And just like water and oil, they can cut it off in a moment's notice.

Our very own military (subsidized by our tax dollars) is in the process of being controlled by these 64 families. A few years ago, I talked to several newly enlisted military men who told me that they are no longer being trained to fight wars and skirmishes overseas; they are being trained to arrest and contain law abiding citizens (without an arrest warrant) here on our own soil when the much anticipated "civil war" of rebellion occurs in response to the takeover by the one-world government. Our own military is being trained to turn against us in the very near future. (I'm not sure if this has continued under the Trump administration. It might have been suspended for a short period. The jury is still out on where the Donald fits in all this. For now, I'm giving him the benefit of the doubt). If one can control the military-- one can control the people! Our military is also spread thin throughout the world just in case the plan of the Globalists to use them here doesn't work. Should our military decide to ignore the orders of the new totalitarian regime, there won't be many of them here on our soil to defend us.

Taxes: We have already touched on the plan to confiscate personal property in a subtle, incremental way through taxes. But I want to insert the following article written by a journalist who makes no claims of being a conservative, but merely states the facts of our present Oligarchical form of government. This was Charley Reese's final column for the Orlando Sentinel. He had been a journalist for 49 years. This is about as clear and easy to understand as it can be. The article below is completely neutral, neither antirepublican nor anti-democrat. Charlie, a retired reporter, has hit the nail directly on the head, defining clearly who it is that in the final analysis must assume responsibility for the judgments made that impact each one of us every day:

545 vs. 300,000,000 People

-By Charlie Reese

"Politicians are the only people in the world who create problems and then campaign against them.

Have you ever wondered, if both the Democrats and the Republicans are against deficits, WHY do we have deficits?

Have you ever wondered, if all the politicians are against inflation and high taxes, WHY do we have inflation and high taxes?

You and I don't propose a federal budget. The President does.

You and I don't have the Constitutional authority to vote on appropriations. The House of Representatives does.

You and I don't write the tax code, Congress does.

You and I don't set fiscal policy, Congress does.

You and I don't control monetary policy, the Federal Reserve Bank does (owned by the 64 elitist families of the NWO! TM).

One hundred senators, 435 congressmen, one President, and nine Supreme Court justices equates to 545 human beings out of the 300 million who are directly, legally, morally, and individually responsible for the domestic problems that plague this country.

I excluded the members of the Federal Reserve Board because that problem was created by the Congress. In 1913, Congress delegated its Constitutional duty to provide a sound currency to a federally chartered, but private, central bank (owned by the Globalist Elites! TM).

I excluded all the special interests and lobbyists for a sound reason. They have no legal authority. They have no ability to coerce a senator, a congressman, or a President to do one cotton-picking thing. I don't care if they offer a politician one million dollars in cash. The politician has the power to accept or reject it. No matter what the lobbyist promises, it is the legislator's responsibility to determine how he votes.

Those 545 human beings spend much of their energy convincing you that what they did is not their fault. They cooperate in this common con regardless of party affiliation.

What separates a politician from a normal human being is an excessive amount of gall. No normal human being would have the gall of a Speaker, who stood up and criticized the President for creating deficits. (The President can only propose a budget. He cannot force the Congress to accept it.).

The Constitution, which is the supreme law of the land, gives sole responsibility to the House of Representatives for originating and approving appropriations and taxes. Who is the Speaker of the House? John Boehner- He is the leader of the majority party. He and fellow House members, not the President, can approve any budget they want. If the President vetoes it, they can pass it over his veto if they agree to. [The House has passed a budget, but the Senate has not approved a budget in over three years. The President's proposed budgets have gotten almost unanimous rejections in the Senate in that time.]

It seems inconceivable to me that a nation of 300 million cannot replace 545 people who stand convicted -- by present facts -- of incompetence and irresponsibility. I can't think of a single domestic problem that is not traceable directly to those 545 people. When you fully grasp the plain truth that 545 people exercise the power of the federal government, then it must follow that what exists is what they want to exist. (Ya' THINK?)

If the tax code is unfair, it's because they want it unfair.

If the budget is in the red, it's because they want it in the red.

If the Army & Marines are in Iraq and Afghanistan it's because they want them in Iraq and Afghanistan (They don't want them on our soil protecting us citizens against our own rogue government! TM).
If they do not receive social security but are on an elite retirement plan not available to the people, it's because they want it that way.

There are no insoluble government problems.

Do not let these 545 people shift the blame to bureaucrats, whom they hire and whose jobs they can abolish; to lobbyists, whose gifts and advice they can reject; to regulators, to whom they give the power to regulate and from whom they can take this power.

Above all, do not let them con you into the belief that there exist disembodied mystical forces like "the economy," "inflation," or "politics" that prevent them from doing what they take an oath to do. (There ARE, however, disembodied forces that are at work in our government. We will discuss that later! TM). Those 545 people, and they alone, are responsible. They, and they alone, have the power. (They are merely loyal puppets, faithfully obeying the commands of the 64 families of the New World Order who deposit millions in their bank accounts! TM).

They, and they alone, should be held accountable by the people who are their bosses (We are supposed to be their bosses). Provided the voters have the gumption to manage their own employees... We should vote all of them out of office and clean up their mess!"

Well stated! Everything we have in our possession is taxed by a bureaucratic government who has submitted to the diabolical plans of the One-world Government:

Tax his land,
Tax his bed,
Tax the table
At which he's fed.

Tax his tractor,
Tax his mule,
Teach him taxes
Are the rule.

Tax his work,
Tax his pay,
He works for
Peanuts anyway.

Tax his cow,
Tax his goat,
Tax his pants,
Tax his coat.

Tax his ties,
Tax his shirt,
Tax his work,
Tax his dirt.

Tax his tobacco,
Tax his drink,
Tax him if he
Tries to think.

Tax his cigars,
Tax his beers,
If he cries,
Tax his tears.

Tax his car,
Tax his gas,
Find other ways
To tax his ass.

Tax all he has
Then let him know
That you won't be done
Til' he has no dough.

When he screams and hollers,
Then tax him some more,
Tax him till
He's good and sore.

Then tax his coffin,
Tax his grave,
Tax the sod in
Which he's laid...

Put these words
Upon his tomb:
'Taxes drove me
To my doom...'

When he's gone,
Do not relax,
It's time to apply
The inheritance tax.
(Author unknown)

Here's a few of the taxes in our "free" country:

Accounts Receivable Tax
Building Permit Tax
Capital Gains Tax
CDL license Tax
Cigarette Tax
Corporate Income Tax
Dog License Tax
Excise Taxes
Federal Income Tax
Federal Unemployment Tax (FUTA)
Fishing License Tax
Food License Tax
Fuel Permit Tax
Gasoline Tax (currently 44.75 cents per gallon)
Gross Receipts Tax
Hunting License Tax
Inheritance Tax
Inventory Tax
IRS Interest Charges
IRS Penalties (tax on top of tax)
Liquor Tax

Luxury Taxes
Marriage License Tax
Medicare Tax
Personal Property Tax
Property Tax
Real Estate Tax
Service Charge Tax
Social Security Tax
Road Usage Tax
Recreational Vehicle Tax
Sales Tax
School Tax
State Income Tax
State Unemployment Tax (SUTA)
Telephone Federal Excise Tax
Telephone Federal Universal Service Fee
Telephone Federal, State and Local Surcharge Taxes
Telephone Minimum Usage Surcharge Tax
Telephone Recurring and Nonrecurring Charges Tax
Telephone State and Local Tax
Telephone Usage Charge Tax
Utility Taxes
Vehicle License Registration Tax

Vehicle Sales Tax

Watercraft Registration Tax

Well Permit Tax

Workers Compensation Tax

World Tax (much of which goes to the United Nations who hate us)

Still think we live in a "FREE SOCIETY?" Not one of these taxes existed 100 years ago, and our nation was the most prosperous in the world. We had absolutely no national debt, had the largest middle class in the world, and Mom stayed home to raise the kids. What in the heck happened? Can you spell 'politicians?' Can you spell "The New World Order Globalists" who own those politicians? Can you spell "property confiscation" and "tyrannical slavery" through excessive taxation?

In summation, even the whole social security tax program, (just like Obamacare), was initiated with the idea in mind of people control. Even though you and I earned that money, they (the Globalists) can refuse to give us that money if we don't willingly submit to their total agenda. They can withhold our own hard-earned money as leverage to coerce us to abide by their tyrannical rules (For example, you must give up all of your guns or receive their micro-chip in your hand before they will mail you your monthly social security check). Possession is nine tenths of the law! And your money is in their hands to do with as they please! (In fact, they are now referring to your social security money as a "government entitlement check").

Public Education-- As a teacher, I observed with great consternation the rapid pace at which the Globalists took over the entire education system. They placed their handpicked people in key positions on the school boards, the school staffs, and in the classrooms of most of the major universities in America. They continue their policies through their own created union called the "National Education Association" (NEA).

They have totally rewritten history books to fit their agenda of destroying anything and everything that smacks of American pride, glory and honor in her sovereign historical heritage. They know that in order to destroy our country, they must erase any semblance of the "free, independent, and sovereign nation" envisioned by our founding fathers.

So books have been replaced, statues have been torn down, museums have been gutted or rearranged, and professors have been hired to promulgate their message of liberal socialism. The philosophical doctrines of "free enterprise" and "capitalism" (which have made us economically strong) have been redefined as "greed" and "arrogance," and have been replaced with words like "political correctness, socialism, redistribution of wealth, and progressivism" -- words which mask the devious and destructive plans and agendas of the Elite Globalists for their final demolition of our Democratic-Republic!

Our schools have become less a place to learn, and more a place to indoctrinate the next generation of Marxist Socialists. They don't want the students to know anything about our true history which includes the "Declaration of Independence" and the "Constitution" because their goal for every student is to make them subservient global citizens, not strong and independent US citizens who can think for themselves. The fact that well over 40 percent of our students are on some type of hypnotic, mind-altering prescription drug can only thrill the Elite in their quest to govern over the masses through mind control. Children today walk around like "zombies" or robots and are mindless guinea pigs and easy prey for the manipulation of the Elite. In fact, the Globalists have a name for these kids and for everyone else they use to accomplish their goals: "Useful Idiots!"

The global Oligarchy already has plenty of money. Yet in a hypocritical fashion and in a sinister twist of irony, they pull the political strings of their pundit puppets in Congress and the educational strings of their liberal cronies in our state universities to continue to indoctrinate Americans with their socialistic message of "redistribution of wealth!" Why? Because they cleverly know that socialism, disguised as "benevolence, fairness, and equality" is the perfect tantalizing bait to entice the "useful idiots" to take the first step toward the inevitable trap that awaits them called global citizenship and totalitarianism-- where they will lose all of their individual rights, liberties, and freedoms. The very things that liberals stand for, rig elections for, protest for, dress up as vaginas for, bash in store windows for, turn over cars for, and even kill students and cops for, are the very things that eventually in the end will erode and eradicate every one of their personal freedoms. But they are too blind to see this! Once the Elite are finished using these "useful idiots" to fulfill their global agenda, they will exterminate most of them.

But the Elitists still have one problem-- nearly 40 percent of American citizens clearly see through their agenda and are not buying what they are selling! So they will continue to indoctrinate our kids in school with their socialistic curriculum which includes revisional history texts as well as their religion of secular humanism and non-scientific evolution (Darwinism: natural selection and survival of the fittest). It won't be long... they will have everyone eating out of their hand (trap)! And no one will bite the hand that feeds them.

Welfare and Healthcare-- This is probably the most useful and prolific tool in the hands of the Elite to secure and maintain "people control!" Their goal has always been to get as many Americans as possible to become totally dependent upon the government (which they own and operate) for food, housing, education and healthcare. This is their best trap! And the history of socialistic experiments in other countries verifies that it always works in the first stage of seducing the people into an eventual and inevitable submission.

Beginning with President Hoover who promised "two cars in every garage and a chicken in every pot," continuing with President Franklin Roosevelt's "New Deal," proceeding with President Johnson's "Great Society," bolstered by President Clinton's "Temporary Assistance for Needy Families Program," and re-enforced by President Obama's irreversible Universal Healthcare Act; these Socialist puppet Presidents of the New World Order effectively implemented redistribution of wealth, killed capitalism, killed free-enterprise, killed economic growth, and increased exponentially the percentage of American citizens dependent upon the government for any type of financial handout/assistance. Not to mention, effectively plunging our Republic into a free fall of financial debt with an ongoing recession from which we will never recover.

In the decade of the fifties, ten percent of the American people were dependent upon the government for food, housing, and healthcare. In the sixties, twenty percent. In the seventies, thirty percent. In the eighties, forty percent. In the nineties, fifty percent. And now? Unofficial estimates surmise that approximately seventy percent of the American people (citizens and non-citizens) are dependent upon the financial resources of our government to provide the essentials they need to survive (including social security). And that's exactly the trend that the Globalist Elites were expecting to develop.

That was their original plan, and they are ecstatic to see that plan successfully moving forward. And by the way, they refer to those Americans who are getting a handout as "Useless Eaters!" Once the Globalists have full control of our nation and the rest of the industrial world, they will begin to mercilessly exterminate all the "Useless Eaters" who at one time depended on them and trusted in them. For now, all the welfare recipients will not bite the hand that feeds them. And they will eventually willingly submit to anything demanded of them by a dictatorial, tyrannical government... even if that means giving up all their rights and freedoms in exchange for food, water, and medicine.

The offices of the President and the Senate: The Elite Globalists pick and choose which candidates they want to place in office in the Senate and in the White House. They want us to think that we are the ones who "vote" them into office, but such is not the case. A few seniors in our High Schools are chosen each year across the nation to become the recipients of a "Rhodes Scholarship" that will give them a free education at one of these Elite-owned universities: Yale, Harvard, Princeton, Cambridge, Columbia. These unsuspecting students are thrilled and "honored" beyond measure for having been picked by the Rhodes family to pursue a law degree from one of these prestigious universities- all expenses paid. They have no clue upon high school graduation that they have been picked by the Globalists to be educated and groomed for the Elites' own future political purposes and agendas. This pool of very sharp students represents both political parties for the appearance of "fairness," but in the process of their education, they are indoctrinated (brainwashed) to become representatives and ambassadors (puppets) of the one-world government Oligarchy. Whether they are Democrats or Republicans, they are groomed to be the next Senators, Presidents, and Federal

Judges. By the time the Elitists think they are ready, the financial backing is in place to hoist these young proteges and "disciples" onto the public stage and into the political campaigns of their respective states to run for Governor, Senator, or Circuit Court Judge. These handpick Republican and Democratic candidates who are practically "owned" by the 64 Global Elitists then run against each other on the same ticket. We go to the polls thinking we are voting for a person who stands for what we believe in and voting against the other candidate whom we think is diametrically opposed to what we believe in; when in reality, both candidates were cut out of the same mold-- globalism! The "opposing" candidates were each picked, educated (indoctrinated), groomed, positioned, propped up and funded by the same people who want to fundamentally change our country from a Democratic/Republic to a "socialistic" third-world country that will willing submit to a global citizenship ruled by one very sinister and powerful dictator.

Think about it! At one time, very few Americans knew anything about Jimmy Carter. But in a few short years he was elected Governor of Georgia, then President of the United States. Little was known of Bill Clinton (indoctrinated at Cambridge University as a "Rhodes Scholar"), but he quickly rose in the ranks of the Elites. Both President Bushes were members of the "Skull and Bones Society" (a subsidiary of the "New World Order") while being indoctrinated and groomed at Yale University. Virtually no one knew who Barrack Obama was when he was a Senator from Chicago. But he became the pride and joy of the Elites who groomed and educated him at Columbia University and quickly sealed every known record about his past including his origin of birth and the history of his immediate family members. Nearly every viable and electable Presidential candidate in my lifetime (both Democrats and Republicans) received their degree from one of the Elite-owned Universities and were members of either the Skull and Bones, the Bohemian Grove, the Free Masons, or the Council on Foreign Relations-- all subsidiaries of the One world government (NWO). There's just way too much in common amongst all of these candidates to simply dismiss it as a ridiculous "conspiracy theory!" They are all puppets whose strings are pulled by the 64 powerful families who want to rule the world!

Every now and then, the Elites will throw the American people a "bone" by allowing a state to elect a conservative to the House of Representatives, knowing that they have already weakened the House to the point that this newly elected man or woman will do no harm to their deceptive agenda. But in the Senate races, they put their Harvard or Yale trained Republican candidate on one ballot to run against their

Harvard or Yale trained Democratic pupil on the other ballot. They sit back with glee as they view the unsuspecting American voters going to the polls to vote one or the other of their puppets into office. They really don't care which one gets in because they are assured that either candidate will be faithful and loyal servants to their political propaganda. But just to be sure, they will continue to drop a few million bucks every now and then into the offshore bank accounts of their willing Republican and Democratic servants.

Before I leave this section of the book, I want to mention the Kennedys and the Clintons and their roles in "global government." The patriarch of the politically powerful Kennedy family was Joseph Kennedy, who supposedly made his millions from "bootlegging" liquor. There's evidence of his close relationship with the Rockefellers and other prominent families of the Elitists. But when three of his sons aspired to climb the political ladder (JFK,

Robert and Teddy), they incrementally attempted to distance themselves from at least the appearance of any close relationship or ties with the original 64 families. When John F. Kennedy was President, he gave a short speech in which he declared:

"The very word 'secret' is repugnant in a free and open society; and we are as a people inherently and historically opposed to secret societies, to secret oaths, to secret proceedings (Free Masons, Bohemian Grove, The Illuminati, Skull and Bones, etc.). We decided long ago that the dangers of excessive and unwarranted concealment of pertinent facts far outweighed the dangers which are cited to justify it.

Today, there is little value in insuring the survival of our nation if our traditions do not survive with it. And there is very grave danger that an announced need for increased security (sealed documents, diminished 1st and 2nd Amendment rights, rigged elections) will be seized upon by those anxious to expand its meaning to the very limits of censorship and concealment (of anything that is not in alignment with the agenda of the New World Order). This very thing (censorship, people control) I do not intend to permit, to the extent that it is in my control (unfortunately, it wasn't in your control; your daddy's friends were pulling the strings and calling the shots of our nation even back then).

And no official of my Administration, whether his rank is high or low, civilian or military, should interpret my words here tonight as an excuse to censor the news, to stifle dissent, to cover up our mistakes, or to withhold from the press and the public the facts they deserve to know (about the attempt of the Elites to control this President's governing authority). For we are opposed around the world by a monolithic and ruthless conspiracy (by the

64 families) that relies on covert means for expanding its sphere of influence (control)-- on infiltration instead of invasion, on subversion instead of free [and unhindered] elections, on intimidation instead of free choice, on guerrillas by night instead of armies by day (their own personally funded wars for people displacement and population reduction). Its preparations are concealed, not published. Its mistakes are buried, not headlined. Its dissenters are silenced, not praised. No expenditure is questioned, no rumor is printed, no secret is revealed. Without debate, without criticism (without a separation of powers by a checks and balance system), no Republic can survive. That is why the Athenian lawmaker Solon decreed it a crime to shrink from controversy.

And that is why our press (news media) is protected by the First Amendment-- the only business in America specifically protected by the Constitution-- not primarily to amuse and entertain, not to emphasize the trivial and sentimental, not to simply give the public what it wants, [and not to editorialize the facts with a left leaning liberal socialistic slant]-- but to inform, to arouse, to reflect, to state our dangers and our opportunities, to indicate our crises and our choices, to lead, mold, educate (with the facts, not opinions), and sometimes even anger public opinion.

This means that government at all levels must meet its obligation to provide you with the fullest possible information outside the narrowest limits of national security.
And so, it is to the printing press [and news media] that we look for strength and assistance, confident that with your help, man will be what he was born to be: free and independent!" (JFK speech to the Press).

President Kennedy gave this speech hoping that the press would be on his side as he was about to expose the evil, sinister takeover plan by the Elite Globalists who falsely concluded that after they had propped him up and got him elected, he would continue to be loyal to them and proceed with the perpetual plan of destroying our Republic. But with this President (as with Nixon and Reagan), they grossly miscalculated. President Kennedy wasn't finished! Here's one of his more specific quotes revealing to us how much he knew about the people who were really pulling his puppet strings and the strings of nearly all our government leaders:

"There is a vast conspiracy by a few politically astute, politically powerful, and financially wealthy families who have as their goal the complete destruction of our nation and the total rule of the world's governments with less than admirable intentions. I am about to expose these people and their agenda very soon!"

Shortly after publicly stating these words,

President John F. Kennedy was assassinated by one of the "mind-controlled" puppets of the Elites' evil regime! JFK discovered that for many years his entire family was being "wined and dined" in a coercive and seductive effort to join the Elites in their destruction of our Republic. John must have reached the point in his political career where he no longer wanted any part of it! John's brother Robert was the next Kennedy to have the opportunity to run for the Presidency. But just like his brother, he knew too much about the "Big Boys" in control and wasn't willing to abide by all their constraining rules. So they "neutralized" him as well! Next, Edward (Teddy) was being groomed by these folks to ascend the political throne as their next presidential puppet. Just like his brothers, he was a willing participant and accomplice in the leftists' deceptive socialistic agenda of higher taxes for the rich (redistribution) in order to continue the "benevolent facade" of feeding the poor, helping the homeless, taking care of the widows and orphans, etc. But also just like his brothers, he stepped out of the circle of the mafia type global "bosses" of the Cabal just long enough to disqualify himself from being a viable, electable candidate. After one unsuccessful effort to run for the office of the Presidency, he was told by them that if he continued to resist them, they would not only make sure he would never become President, but more dire consequences would be forthcoming! He got the message, kept his mouth shut, minded his own business and remained their loyal liberal Senator puppet and accomplice for the remainder of his career.

The Kennedys knew too much! Information is power-- but too much information about the secret plans of more powerful people will not only make one vulnerable to those very people, but a lifelong slave to them. Even though the Kennedy brothers were members of the Illuminati, they mistakenly thought that their family was powerful enough, influential enough, and wealthy enough to successfully resist the Global Elitists' efforts to control their every move and policies. Their abrupt deaths proved them wrong! Beginning way back in the decade of the sixties, the message by the group of 64 Globalists was clear and non-negotiable: Get in line with us.... our die! As you yourself said in your speech, Mr. President, "Its dissenters are silenced!" Many members of the Kennedy family were associated with the "Illuminati" (the "enlightened ones"), a subsidiary of the New World Order Global Government. They were in way over their heads. They knew too much! Some wanted out! But obviously, it doesn't work that way!

Bill and Hillary Clinton are definitely puppets of the Elitists. Bill attended Cambridge as a "Rhodes' Scholar" where he was groomed and propped up to become a future President. By posturing himself as a "Southern Baptist church goer," he was able to deceive the good ole boys and girls of Arkansas and secure enough "centrist" votes to be elected as their Governor. I lived in southern Missouri and taught in a school in Branson near the Arkansas border where I met hundreds of citizen voters from this beautiful state south of mine. None of them voted for Clinton! And out of the thousands of their acquaintances, they knew of no one who voted for him. They were unanimously convinced that election fraud had propelled Slick Willy to quick prominence in the heart of one of the Bible belts of America.

While Governor, Bill was part of a covert operation that allowed billions of dollars of cocaine to enter the USA through the small town of Mena. (There is documented evidence that the world-wide production, marketing, and distribution of cocaine actually assisted in the funding of the Global Cabal). When someone in his administration (and in some cases, outside of his inner circle) discovered what was happening and planned to come forward with their information, they were killed; and their deaths were set up to look like "accidents" or "suicides!" There were forty dead bodies surrounding the Clinton gubernatorial administration. But that was just the beginning.

As a puppet and servant of the Elitists, Bill campaigned for the Presidency as a political "centrist." He was clearly the handpicked one to replace George H. W. Bush, with whom the Elite were finished using to accomplish their goals. Just to make certain that their puppet (Bill) would become the next President, they threw another puppet into the mix named "Ross Perot" (whom no one had ever heard of) to split the votes of the Republican Party and seal the deal for their next loyal puppet President-- Bill Clinton! I watched the debates between the three. It was obvious to me that their plan was working because George had no energy, no enthusiasm, no political strategies, no principled platform, and seemingly no desire to continue as President. He already knew going into the campaign and the debates that his bosses had picked Bill to succeed him. He was instructed by them to go through the process (the dog and pony show) to give the illusion of a "free and fair election" in a "democratic" society. Just as many predicted, Ross Perot split the conservative votes and assured the democratic candidate a sound victory. Without their puppet Ross, Bush would have soundly defeated their puppet Bill.

Wouldn't have mattered anyway who was elected. All three were owned by the Globalists. But Clinton was their man for the job now!   And they used him in their continued efforts to run our government for the next eight years and fundamentally erode more of our rights and liberties with higher taxes and a stronger centralized federal government-- all under the illusion of a "free and independent society." All under the guise of a Democratic/Republic!

Many believe that the Clinton marriage was arranged for political purposes only. Some who have worked for both of them as body guards have stated that she is a practicing lesbian who detests her pretend" husband. And he is a whorehound" womanizer who doesn't give a flip about what she or anyone else thinks about his many adulterous affairs. In fact, this was the way it was set up by the Elite who gave each of them permission to privately live separate lives and pursue whatever made them happy in private sexual relationships. They were (and still are) so popular with the deceived American people that their murders and sexual perversions were inconsequential. The American people just didn't care!

Bill has been observed attending the meetings of the Bohemian Grove and the Bilderbergs. The first group is the "spiritual" arm of the Globalists. The second is the "political" extension. And the research of many has concluded that

Hillary is connected with the "enlightened ones" of the demonic organization called the Illuminati. Here's a brief look at the Clinton's political resume:

12 rape accusations
121 mysterious deaths (sacrificing the few for the good of the many)
1 dead American ambassador
3 Navy Seals dead
10 investigations
1 impeachment
2 disbarments
30,000+ emails deleted to hinder a federal investigation
Helped create and arm ISIS by political decisions made as Secretary of State

If these crimes would have been committed 80 years ago, these folks would have spent the rest of their lives in prison. But this couple has always been (and forever shall be) protected by the Globalists who put them in office!

7

The Illuminati

As the Bilderbergs, the Council on Foreign Relations, the Trilateral Commission, the European Union, the United Nations, and the Unites States government are the "political" entities or extenders of the Globalist New World Order; and the World Bank, the Bank of London, the oil companies, the pharmaceutical companies, and the cocaine industry are the "economic" resources and conduits of the Cabal; so are the World Council of Churches, the Bohemian Grove, the Free Masons, the Skull and Bones, and the Illuminati the religious or "spiritual" branches of these power hungry tyrants who are jockeying for position and power to control the entire world. My research has uncovered the covert activities of the "One-worlders" in their pursuit of the spirit world to assist them in their quest for world dominance.

A segment of this 64 family covert operation is interacting with and receiving knowledge and power from unseen disembodied spirits which they call "extraterrestrials" or "higher powers" or "enlightened ones" or "ascended masters" whom the Elitists deceptively believe will compassionately lift all of us up out of the disgusting, debilitating, and decadent world of poverty, disease, political and cultural divisions, upheavals, wars, evil capitalism, repugnant free enterprise, and the "failed" experiments of the "oppressive" forms of governments such as our very own Democratic/Republic. The Globalists are blindly convinced that with the assistance of these "otherworldly" creatures-- this "supernatural race"-- they can unify the entire world under a religious form of ecumenicalism that will ultimately usher in the utopian government of "world peace, world safety, world unity and prosperity for all!" But this is just their sales propaganda to disguise their ultimate sadistic and subversive plan for totalitarianism. The instructions and powers they are receiving are not from the God of Holy Writ-- but from satan himself!

One of the political "darlings" or "princesses" of the Globalists is Hillary Clinton. I read about an interview way back in the late eighties in which she admitted to communicating with the dead spirits of Eleanor Roosevelt (wife of President FDR) and Mahatma Gandhi on a daily basis to receive her wisdom, knowledge, and instruction for her personal life and her political philosophies and ideologies. By her own words in the interview, she was convinced she was interacting with the "ghosts" of Eleanor and Gandhi who were "down-loading" invaluable information and power in preparing her to be a future leader of our nation and the world. She called these demons her "spirit guides." When asked if she ever consulted Jesus, she replied, "That's too personal!"

First of all, the Bible specifically states that when our spirits leave our bodies at death, they are immediately ushered to one of two places-- and the earthly realm is not one of those places. According to God's Word, there is no such thing as "ghosts"! Only disembodied spirits called "demons" who have the ability to mimic a deceased person in appearance and in voice are roaming the earthly realm. Hillary was clearly interacting with the powers of darkness-- not the ghosts of Eleanor or Gandhi.

Secondly, God warns us in His Word to never communicate with the dead (the spirit world). That forbidden practice is called "necromancy," and God knew that if we curiously interfaced with these evil spirits, we would be conjuring up the demonic world of darkness that would eventually possess us and destroy us. God also warned us to never go to any other "source" other than Himself for knowledge, information, instruction, healing, or power. He calls this interaction with the spirit world "witchcraft, sorcery, and idolatry!" But Hillary and all the others in these secret luciferian societies snub their arrogant and defiant noses at the true God who created them and instead pursue the powers of darkness who in exchange for their very souls promise these members of the Elite the powers they covet to rule the world.

Hillary Clinton wrote a thesis in college praising the political and philosophical doctrines of Saul Alinsky-- a luciferian who was a proponent of a one-world government with a one-world religion. This "hero" mentor of Hillary was an unashamed worshipper of satan, filled with the very same demons that spoke to Mrs. Clinton and gave her their "wisdom" and instructions for governmental policies on a daily basis. Alinsky dedicated one of his books (Rules for Radicals) to the "master of his soul" -- satan. Hillary glorified this book.

The phrase "ascended masters" is often used by the New Agers and the Unity Universalist Unitarian Church when they refer to those unseen spiritual entities who give them wisdom and power. We Christians know that biblically speaking, these "masters" are in fact demons who will quickly possess and ultimately destroy anyone willing to invite them into their souls.

Hillary also holds in high esteem the controversial Margaret Sanger, a Globalist whose outrageous racial policies of population control are adherently embraced and followed by many liberals today. Margaret established organizations which morphed and evolved into Planned Parenthood, the organization that to this day butcher babies in the womb and sells their body parts for "scientific experiments" under the guise of "cloning" and "stem cell research." Margaret used her influence (and "powers") to persuade Congress to create a "Parliament of Population Control" to control and curtail the population through "birth rates" and "immigration" policies not unlike the "survival of the fittest" religion of Hitler's regime. As with Hitler, she wanted to produce a "superior race" of "highly intelligent" and "superbly enlightened" human beings. Like the government of China today, this was to be accomplished through "birth-control" methods of abortion and "sterilization." She had the audacity to call the various methods of birth-control (killing unborn babies), "defending the unborn against their own potential disabilities." She is also quoted as saying, "We don't want the word to get out that we want to exterminate the entire negro race."

African Americans today have no clue that their darling princess Hillary who claims to champion each of their causes is in fact wanting to eradicate their entire race because their "inferior" race and culture just doesn't fit into the plan of the Elitists to develop a superior race of brilliant "demagogues" who in their supernatural wisdom and knowledge will rule the world. The Elites (including Hillary) are merely using these black "useful idiots" to get elected-- just as Bill deceitfully used Hillary and the institution of marriage to give the illusion that they were a typical southern American "Christian" family who has the American people's best interest in mind! The Clinton and Obama administrations were the most delusional and deceptive fraud ever imposed upon the American people. But this plan of the Globalists unfolded precisely according to their sinister agenda to ensure the final death blow of our Republic. It was successful! The American people had been magnificently snookered. And it wouldn't be the last time of their willingness to be bewitched!

It has been documented that the Bohemian Grove was started by the stage actor, Henry "Harry" Edwards in California back in 1872. This "secret society" has become arguably the most prolific arm of the Illuminati! Both Republican and Democratic Congressmen, Presidents, and Federal Judges have been associated with this demonic organization for many decades. We now know that every Republican President since 1923 has either been a member or has had a close relationship with this devilish "secret fraternal society!" Even the likes of Richard Nixon, Ronald Reagan, the Bushes, Colin Powell, Dick Cheney, and many others have been photographed during their attendance and/or involvement with the meetings of this subsidiary male-only fraternity of the One-world government, where they make animal and human sacrifices to the demonic "owl god" of knowledge, wisdom, and information. This "all-seeing" and "all-knowing" demon-god is held in the highest regard by our government leaders in a similar fashion as the all-seeing "eye" designed by the Free Masons on the pyramid of our paper money. There continues to be a close relationship of the members of the Skull and Bones Society, the Bohemian Grove, and the Free Masons with the Illuminati, since they are all in affiliation with the Globalist Cabal.

I have been acquainted with many so called "Christians" (some even Pastors) who are proud members of the Free

Masons. They are quick to relate to me that one of the symbols of this religious organization is the Bible. They are also quick to argue that their organization does a lot of good in their respective communities. They relate how they are comforted with this newly discovered "brotherhood" that meets all their needs for community and fellowship. However, they soon find out that when they are called upon to pray, they are forbidden to invoke the name of Jesus. And as they climb the structural levels of secretive powers and authority, they are "enlightened" with the realization that the "God" they had for years been acknowledging in their prayers is none other than Lucifer himself!

The Free Masons have a history that they claim goes all the way back to King Solomon. In reality, this demonic organization has its roots in Egyptian and Babylonian paganism. An honest inquiry would conclude that their foundational tenets are rooted in eastern, paganist occultism (much like the Bohemian Grove and the Skull and Bones Society). Many surmise that here on American soil, this demonic organization was established and funded by the Rothschild family in 1731. Many of the signers of our "Declaration of Independence" were Free Masons. The government buildings in Washington, DC were designed and laid out by the Free Masons (including the statue on top of the capitol building). Our freshly printed paper money today was designed by the Masons during Franklin D. Roosevelt's presidency. The pyramid, the "all-seeing eye," and the Latin phrase "Novus Ordo Seclorum," which interpreted is "A New Order of the Ages," were all added with the intent of introducing "The New Deal of the Ages," i.e., the New World Order.

Many, if not most of our Presidents, Congressmen, and Federal Judges in the past and present belonged to this powerful organization that is owned and funded by the Global Elites. It would take many books to list them all. But here are a few notable names:

George Washington (33rd degree Mason)
Thomas Jefferson
Benjamin Franklin
James Monroe
J. Edgar Hoover (FBI)
Earl Warren (Chief Justice of the Supreme Court)
President Jimmy Carter (33rd degree Mason)
Senator Jesse Helms ("conservative" from N.C.- 33rd degree Mason)
Senator Storm Thurmond ("conservative" from S.C.)
Senator Orrin Hatch ("conservative" from Utah)
Rev. Jesse Jackson (liberal Presidential candidate)

These are just a few of the names of the many past and present leaders of our nation who not only belonged to this dark and deceptive organization but were high ranking and powerful members. Many leaders today in both political parties are members as well. One cannot be a thirty-third degree Mason without being privy to the information about the New World Order of the Elites, and the powers of darkness that control them! They know everything! And they are intricately involved as the principal players in the selling out and the devious destruction of our once great Republic.

Some of our politicians may give the illusion that they are "Christian conservatives" in order to get elected, but their association with these demonic organizations reveals their real motives of governmental power and exposes their true financial interests in gaining wealth in exchange for their cooperation with the "Big Boys" at the top! They've sold their souls to the devil himself! And they've sold us out to a world government whose primary goal is to make us serfs in their feudal system, and "neutralize" those of us who are unwilling to cooperate with their efforts to force us to submit to their totalitarian regime.

I cannot leave the discussion of the spiritual, religious branches of the One world government without mentioning the space program. President Harry S. Truman was instructed by the Globalists to form a "secret" committee whom he called the "MJ-12" (the Majestic 12 or the Magical 12). This committee of scientists and astronauts were instructed by our President to investigate all matters pertaining to the celestial world of "extraterrestrials!" Reports were coming in to the government at an alarming rate of many sightings and interactions of US citizens with the "grays" (the name used to describe space aliens or "Martians"). The consistency and the credibility of a vast number of citizens, along with the persistent pressure on the government for answers gave opportunity to the Elitists to present in their own way and by their own spin the reality and purpose of the visits of these strange entities from outer space. Our government had already been interfacing with the demonic world for many decades, when another Globalist puppet named Eisenhower became our President. He was so curious about this covert space committee and their research that he continued to fund and expand this God-forbidden correlation with the spirit world. According to his own great granddaughter in an interview years later, Eisenhower had heard about our government interfacing with these "grays" from another world and wanted to observe these meetings. He flew to Colorado where he was involved in the communications between the Globalists in our government and the demonic spirits in satan's dark kingdom, believing these entities to be the "enlightened ones" who will soon assist the humans on our planet to achieve a utopian "nirvana" which will usher in a superior race of humans who will then bring about "world peace and unity!" This new race of humans will be indwelt by and empowered with these spiritual aliens "for the good of mankind!" Many who have researched this satanic plan of our government funded by our tax dollars have concluded that scientific knowledge and skills have been passed down from these evil spirits to the governments of the earth to create humanlike robots (reptilians), flying machines, satellites, and even nuclear bombs.

Suffice it to say, most of NASA's rockets have been sent up for the purpose of placing orbiting satellites to interface with the spirit world as well as to spy on us. Everyone knows that the technology is in place in space for our own government to hear our every conversation and to know our every geographical move. The reasons or excuses our government leaders give us concerning these satellites and the microchips they read in our televisions, cars, phones, and bank cards is never the truth. We are told that this surveillance, made possible by micro-chips, is for our own good-- for our own safety and protection!

Your TV has a chip in it that allows your government to watch and hear everything you do and say-- even if your TV is turned off! Your car, your phone, your iPad, your computer, and your credit cards have chips in them so the Globalists can monitor your every move and bank transactions-all possible with the Space satellites that the Globalist-sanctioned organization called "NASA" has launched and orbited. And all funded by the taxes of the "useful idiots" called "U.S. citizens!"

Still think you are living in a "free" country? Still think that you have any semblance of privacy left? Still believe you can live an unobtrusive life, free from any governmental interference or constraints?

Still think that we live in a "Democratic/Republic" where the government has our best interests in mind? Don't be delusional! The old America is dead. It was killed long ago.... by design!

8

The Media and the Movie Industry

It has become blatantly obvious that our newspapers and media news have ceased merely reporting the facts and have transitioned to editorializing the day-to-day events of our nation and the entire world. The Globalists own nearly every television news network and every major newspaper corporation in this nation. Through their own printed page and their cable and satellite media, they have maximized their efforts to create the conundrum whereby we only read or hear what they want us to read or hear and arrive at the predetermined conclusions of their own making. Their many slanted spins and contortions of the facts are just another form of hypnotic "Global-speak!" Not many decades ago, there was but one editorial page in every newspaper, and one editorial journalist on each TV news segment. Now, the entire paper and all the media news networks are one big editorial deception. The sad part of this is that their predictions and calculations that most Americans will not see through their propaganda have been proven to be incredibly accurate. There are a myriad of examples of "fake news" promulgated by the one-worlders. But I won't take the space or time to discuss these here.

The Globalist Elites have wormed their way into the movie industry in an incredulous manner by releasing and supplying their seemingly endless financial resources. Hollywood is now practically owned by the 64 family Elitists. The Illuminati branch of this sadistic government has influenced the writers, producers, directors and even the actors of our film industry to solidify their ideals and agendas of creating an attitude and an atmosphere that will enhance their idea of a "new spirituality." Nearly every Disney movie in my lifetime has components that propagate their subtle "New Age" spirituality of higher enlightenment and super-natural powers. (Walt Disney himself was a Free Mason and a Globalist). The demonic arts and crafts of witchcraft and sorcery are deceitfully and delicately woven into every theme. Over the past four decades, I have noticed the manner in which the Globalists have incrementally desensitized the American people by including supernatural beasts, demons, and many "other-worldly" characters in their films. The movie "ET" is an example of their presentation to the American people of the extra-terrestrials who are here to communicate with us, help us, infuse their supernatural wisdom and powers to us, encourage us, and take us to the next level of enlightenment. The demon spirit "ET" was clothed with a peaceful, benevolent "face" to seduce the unsuspecting and undiscerning movie watcher into believing that all extraterrestrials are indeed harmless, peace-loving creatures. "Close Encounters of the Third Kind" was another of their desensitizing efforts to prepare our world for the eventual invasion of "sympathetic" aliens (demons). "Men in Black" reveals how our government agencies are already interacting with these "harmless and silly little creatures!" The movie "Star Wars" was their tool to synthesize or infuse the material world with the spirit world with the introduction of one mysterious "force" or energy containing within itself a "good side" and a "bad side" (Yin and Yang). "The Matrix" was written, funded and produced by the Globalists to blur the line between the world of empiricism and the ethereal world of illusion, leaving the viewer with the challenge of deducing which one is truly the reality. Whether it is an "innocent", child-oriented Warner Brothers' film series called "Harry Potter" where the demonic arts of witchcraft and sorcery are portrayed as harmless pranks, or the many "R-rated" adults only movies, the Elitists in Hollywood have been successful in propelling their agenda of socialism, reincarnation/animal worship ("Lion King"), New Age ("Star Wars"), spiritual evolution, and a new "enlightened" human race of the future with supernatural wisdom and powers. The members of the Globalist Illuminati continue to be successful in brain-washing the vulnerable citizens of the United States through the movie industry. And by the way, they not only fund the movies, they "own" the actors as well. Many popular actors and actresses are members of the demonic religion called "Scientology," founded by L. Ron Hubbard. John Travolta, Tom Cruise, Michele Miscavige, Kristie Alley are among many in the movie industry who are fully committed to this demonic religion funded by the Globalists. Allister Crowley and Anton LaVey, both self-proclaimed satan worshippers are also members of this dark subsidiary religion of the New World Order called "Scientology!"

Hollywood has implemented and synchronized religious and spiritual overtones of Hinduism, reincarnation, metaphysics, witchcraft, sorcery, spells, incantations, transgenderism, and New Age demonism into many of their films. Coincidence? Hardly! The Globalists are even behind the Disney produced films, deceptively catering to the next generation of children to indoctrinate them and desensitize them to the spirit world.

The present Pope and his world-wide Roman Catholic Church, the very politically and theologically liberal World Council of Churches, the American Council of Churches, the New Age Movement Church called "Unity Unitarian Universalists" and the world-wide ecumenical movement unifying all faiths and religions under one umbrella is the agenda of the Globalist family of 64. And they are using the film and entertainment industry as one of their tools to accomplish their goals. Pope Francis is thought by many (even Catholics) to be the "Black Pope" or the last Pope who is the "False Prophet" mentioned in the book of Revelation. In his seductive and deviant quest to unify all faiths, he is propagating antibiblical and demonically-inspired New Age philosophies in many of his speeches. The merging of "Christianity" and Islam is another of their ploys to bring all religions under the dictates and control of this evil, central world government. Many will discover soon enough that the true

"Pastor" of this Global religion is none other than satan himself. And that is precisely the reason that the true followers of Jesus will never embrace this ecumenical one-world religion.

9

The New World Order

Every President since Teddy Roosevelt has used the term "New World Order" in at least one speech. Coincidence? I think not! Both Republican and Democratic Presidents have initiated policies and/or signed bills into law that have eroded our individual freedoms and liberties to the point that this New World Order has easily and incrementally ensconced itself into our nation...incognito. This infiltration of a global government has successfully yet deceptively masqueraded as "safety, protection, peace, prosperity, and unity!" Fourteen Presidents since Teddy have called for or supported a "League of Nations" to "defend" us against our foreign enemies. This "League" eventually morphed into the present "United Nations," funded by billions of our tax dollars annually. It is estimated that the United States citizens' tax dollars have supported this "baby" of the New World Order to the tune of trillions of dollars since its conception. The serfs of the global feudal system in America have been snookered again to finance the very organization that hates us and is working toward a one-world government, run by the anti-American Elitists!

For there to be a "new order," there must first be the death of the "old order!" There can be no introduction and infiltration of the "new" without first destroying the "old." The very words "New World Order" deceptively disguise the eventual tyrannical government of totalitarianism. "New" sounds so adventurous and so warm and welcoming! "World" sounds so unifying, and so universally and culturally sophisticated. "Order" sounds so methodical, so securely regimented, and so safe and protective! But the whole thing is deceptively evil! The Globalists will continue to create "disorder" in our nation to birth and finalize their subversive "new order!"

I recall several decades ago when then President Bill Clinton gave a speech on TV in which he said, "Sometimes, we have to sacrifice the few-- for the good of the many!" I just about came out of my chair because I recognized this very principle and these very words in "The Communist Manifesto" written by Karl Marx. Not long after this Clinton speech, the Secretary of Commerce Ron Brown was killed in an "unfortunate" plane crash, along with several hundred American citizens on a commercial jet. John F. Kennedy Jr. was also killed in an "accidental" plane crash.

Both Brown and Kennedy knew much about the New World Order, the Illuminati, and the Global family of 64. They also carried much information about the murders by the Clintons. JFK Jr. was leading in the polls and was a shoe-in to become the next Senator for New York. But his plane went down, assuring Hillary the victory. The words, "sacrifice the few for the good of the many" is nothing more than sinister double-speak and evil global speak terminology, meaning it's OK to kill a few innocent people in order to move forward with policies that will eventually "benefit" the masses. But in reality, they are saying that it's okay to murder a few innocent people along with those few rogue individuals who know too much and can no longer be trusted with such valuable information. In their minds, it's the "right" thing to do to kill a few innocent

Americans in order to bring the whole world under the control of the Global Government.

Sacrificing (butchering) the few for the "good" of the many means it's OK for the Globalists to kill millions of unborn babies under the guise of "family planning" and "population control."

Sacrificing the few for the "good" of the many means eradicating an entire "inferior" race by "purging the undesirables" so the superior race can appear and rule the earth. (Margaret Sanger)

Sacrificing the few for the "good" of the many means sending our boys overseas to fight a war that we were forbidden by the Globalists to win (Vietnam, Korean, Iraq, Kuwait, Afghanistan)!

Sacrificing the few for the "good" of the many means allowing our soldiers to die when under attack in Benghazi (under orders by Secretary of State, Hillary Clinton).

Sacrificing the few for the "good" of the many means it's okay for the Globalists to brainwash a mentally unstable kid to go into a school and kill a few students so that in a fit of anger, rage, and disgust the whole nation will demand that our government disarm its law-abiding citizens, paving the way for criminals to ignore the new gun laws and continue their murderous ways! And paving the way for the final takeover by the Globalists of our disarmed and defenseless nation.

Sacrificing (killing) the few for the "good" of the many means it's okay to kill anyone who might expose the evil plans of the Globalists working through our government to destroy our once great Republic.

To these wicked Globalists, "sacrificing the few for the good of the many" might even mean that they would feel morally justified in planning and executing the assassination of our current President-- if they deemed it a "good" thing for the American people and for the full implementation of their Global agenda. They have certainly done this before.

Sacrificing the few for the "good" of the many means it's OK to kill the Republic of the United States of America in order to achieve the greater and more noble plan of implementing the One-World government! The "New World Order" proponents in our government believe they are morally and ethically justified in supporting and sustaining the abortion industry to accomplish their three-fold agenda:

Depopulation- in order to manage a sustainable number of "useful idiots." Obliterating all inferior races (including the black race) and getting rid of potential "useless eaters!"

Stem-cell research- for the genetic engineering and cloning of a superior race of humans (just like what Hitler wanted).

The gargantuan Globalists feel morally righteous in funding the movie and video industries to produce violent movies and games that will induce more riots, cop killings, school shootings, and domestic violence. They know that out of this designed chaos will come the final dismantling of the Second Amendment as well as the eradication of more individual freedoms and liberties. And when the riotous chaos hits their desired climax, they will finally have their excuse for "martial law" which will in effect be the final death knell of all our once cherished freedoms. Out of the conception of their strategically designed "disorder"... they get to birth their long-awaited baby called "new order."

The existentialism of these Globalists will stop at no evil they deem to be "good" for the full implementation of their desired end. They define that which is "good" as being "evil;" and that which is "evil" as being "good!"

It is an "evil" thing in the state of Maine to harvest a pregnant lobster. So they impose a thousand-dollar fine but continue to encourage and fund the "good" killings of humans in the womb! In most states, it is a thousand dollar fine, the confiscation of your gun and vehicle, and the confinement of three days in jail for the harvesting of a deer or turkey out of the prescribed hunting season. This activity is deemed by the Globalist social engineers in those state governments as being very "evil." But in those same states, they will financially subsidize the crushing of the skull and the dismembering of the body parts of your pre-born baby.

In some states, if you run over a possum with your car, and that ugly critter had babies on its back, you are fined $500.00. If you kill an alligator, you are fined $1,000! If you damage, destroy, or just simply remove the eggs of a wild turkey from its nest, you will be $1,000 poorer! But you can kill the baby in your womb because that is morally and ethically acceptable-- even encouraged! Remember, to them-- good is evil... and evil is good!

Abortion will never be overturned because it was instigated by both the Democratic and Republican Globalists in our government, and forever solidified by our Globalist Supreme Court. The Wall around our southern borders will never be built because the New World Order proponents in our government want the continued influx of illegal immigrants to flow across our borders to accelerate the destruction of our cultural, political, historical, and economic infra- structure.

The Globalist puppets calling the shots in our government would never dare to stifle the illegal drug industry or even closely regulate the prescription drug industry because they not only get hefty financial "kickbacks" for turning the other way, but understand fully how the drug companies and the illegal drug cartels fund their very own New World Order bosses, who in turn reward them handsomely for their loyal submission. The Globalists desire more than anything for every American to be addicted to mind-altering prescription drugs that produce the hypnotic effect of mindless zombies or robots, willing to submit to even the most tyrannical laws of the New World Order.

So I present to the American people your "New World Order" in Washington, DC! Pretending to pass laws for your "good!" Pretending to be the champions of your greatest concerns! Pretending to be ambassadors and bastions of freedom and democracy. Pretending to guard and protect you. And continuing to feed you, clothe you, house you, educate you, and subsidize your businesses. All the while over-taxing you to the point of confiscating your property. All the while encouraging illegal immigration. All the while subsidizing "sanctuary cities" with your tax dollars to protect the illegal thugs crossing our borders who want to drug and rape your daughters and kill those who don't agree with their religion. All the while financially supporting the illegals who hate our country with a check in the amount of $30,000 per year for food, housing and healthcare; while allowing our war veterans to go hungry and homeless. All the while selling you out to the sinister plans of the dictatorial Global government. All the while orchestrating the final blows to blatantly kill what was once the greatest nation on earth! And all the while planning to eventually "neutralize" you, because after all, you are nothing more to them than an inferior "useful idiot," a "useless eater," a "feudal serf," and soon-- a "needless liability!" For now, the New World Order which includes our "elected" officials will gladly steal your money through taxes until they have no more use for you.

10
The Donald Factor

Where and how does President Trump fit into all of this? We know that every President (Republican and Democratic) for the past 80 years has been a willing puppet of the Elite-64 family Globalists. We know without any doubt that the Bushes, the Clintons, and the Obamas were willing puppets of the NWO who were used to continue the process of destroying our Republic with their liberal, socialistic global policies. But what about The Donald? Does he belong to them too? Is he also controlled by the Elitists? Or is he truly an outsider who honestly thinks he can reverse the policies of the One-world government that have been securely in place for many decades?

There's no doubt in my mind that before the last elections, the next puppet President of the NWO was supposed to be Hillary. The blatant and brazen election fraud in the democratic primaries was rigged to ensure her victory. The documented cases of election fraud in the presidential election was put in place by the Globalists to ensure a victorious outcome for their darling princess. But she lost! Her defeat put a temporary "monkey wrench" in their agenda and slowed down their speedy train for the final destructive blow of our Republic. I say "slowed down" because I believe that as long as the

Globalist puppets of both political parties are in control of Congress, of the FBI, of the CIA, and of every Federal Court, they will continue to have their way as they will effectually block every single thing that Trump wants to do in his attempt to return us to an independent, sovereign nation again.

The jury is still out on whether or not Trump is controlled by the Elitists, or whether or not he will eventually cave to their desires (or threats). But as for now, it seems as though they hate him with a passion. Every single liberal in the news media hates him. Every single liberal Democrat and many Globalist Republicans in the Senate hate him. They not only hate him with a passion, they abhor and despise him! And would probably not mind at all if their Elite Bosses arranged the same "neutralization" procedures for Trump that they successfully enacted and executed for JFK.

When Trump was miraculously elected, my conservative Christian friends celebrated with glee. They truly believed that he would single-handedly return our country to its former glory days as a bona-fide Republic, with its Judeo-Christian roots! I knew that his hands would be tied! I knew that the Globalists had already infiltrated and saturated every single **tier** and level of our government. I knew that even if Trump used the "power of the pen" in by-passing the liberals in his to attempt to enforce "executive orders," he would be met with opposition by our liberal, global puppets in the Federal Courts. Obama by-passed Congress many times with his executive orders and not one of them was overturned by the liberal courts. Trump has tried to implement sound principles by the fiat of executive orders but has had them repeatedly stricken down by those in our courts who want our Republic destroyed from within and want the New World Order to be in full control here on our own soil.

There are a few things, though, that have me somewhat puzzled about Trump. First, he is a very intelligent man who does his research. So he had to know about the infiltration of the Globalists in our government long before he ran for office. But perhaps just like their puppet JFK, maybe Trump had the boldness and audacity to think he could fight them, relinquish their grip and control on our nation, and put us back on the track of free enterprise and capitalism; sovereignty and independence; freedom and liberty. If his strengths in his vision for America were his boldness, his tenacity, and his resolve; his weakness was his miscalculation of the widespread saturation of the socialistic New World Order puppets and proponents at every level of the three branches of our government. He sincerely thought he could drain the swamp. But he didn't calculate just how deep and wide the swamp truly is!

The second thing that concerns me is Trump's passion to negotiate a "peace treaty" between Israel and her Arab Muslim enemies. Several times in his presidential campaign, Trump promised to complete the negotiations and the signing of this treaty that no other President has been able to successfully enact. Every single President before Trump has tried but failed to create an agreeable treaty between Israel and her surrounding neighbors. Trump assured us that his son-n-law, Jared Kushner (a Jew) would successfully negotiate and secure a treaty between the sworn enemies of the Middle East for the first time in many centuries.

The Bible says that in the "last days" right before the return of Christ, a seven-year treaty or covenant of peace between Israel and her enemies would be signed by a world leader who would then break that covenant in the middle of the seven years. That world leader would be promoted to power by the global government (NWO).

He is referred to in the Bible has "the antichrist" who is filled with the powers of darkness (the "enlightened ascended masters"; the "extra-terrestrials"). If Trump and Kushner are successful with this seven-year treaty, that is definitely a "game changer" in the whole reason why and how God put him into the White House-- against all human odds.

To most true followers of Christ, President Obama has all the personality traits, the powers, the persuasiveness, the cultic following of the masses, and the deceptive, fraudulent influences of a prototype of the anti-christ. Obama twice deceived the American people to get elected. Then proceeded to have his way in every single socialistic policy to destroy our nation while both houses of Congress and the judges in our federal courts were in a deep, hypnotic, slumberous sleep. He continues to be the leader of a shadow government (NWO) in Washington and continues to be very popular on a world-wide scale. He aspires to be the next Secretary General of the United Nations and had even been the de-facto President of the Globalist European Union at one point during his presidency. But if Trump and Kushner can pull this treaty off, they will be the new "heroes" of the world, accomplishing what no other world leader has ever come close to accomplishing. And according to the Scriptures, one of them would assume the position as the ultimate world leader called the anti-christ!

Most true Christians who know the prophesies of the Bible concerning the description of the last political world leader would not be surprised if Obama was "the one" who rose to global power as the anti-christ. Many would not even be shocked if Kushner was the one. But if Trump turned out to be the very one spoken of in God's Word who will rule the world for seven years, it would be a complete mental and spiritual paradigm shift in the lives of both those who have always hated him, and those who elected him to the political office of President.

No doubt that God used Trump to successfully relocate the Capitol of Israel from Tel Aviv to Jerusalem to set up the politically prophesied structuring of the "end of times" in the Middle East. Israel exhibited their appreciation to him in this important move by engraving his picture on one of their "commemorative coins." He has shown himself to be their trusted friend... for now! But will he gradually turn against them in the end? We shall see! Will we continue to see the perpetual demise and seemingly inevitable destruction of our Republic by the Globalist New World Order under Trump? Or like dogs, will we have a temporary reprieve, enjoying a few of the "bones" thrown our way by the Globalists such as the recent minuscule tax cuts. We shall see!

In the mean-time:

Trump wants to protect Americans by building a wall to prevent the drug runners and murderers from coming illegally into our country. The Globalists in both Houses of Congress don't want that wall! So they call Trump a "racist" as a political weapon in their deceptive plans to stop the wall from ever being built.

Trump wants to defund the sanctuary cities that protect illegals from any and all repercussions of any of their illegal activities. The Globalist Congressmen (and women) in both Parties WANT the sanctuary cities to protect the non-citizen criminals. So they continue to fund them-- against the wishes of the majority of Americans.

Trump wants to end the unfair trade agreements between the US and China (and Mexico)! The Globalist Republicans and Democrats don't want any changes here either! Because it would deter their plan to add to the soaring deficit and bankrupt America.

Trump wants to significantly cut our national debt of twenty trillion by cutting welfare payments to illegal immigrants who for decades have contributed to driving the debt to an outrageous and dangerous high! The Globalists view this desire by Trump to be a "racist" ploy against all foreigners! So they will continue to fight him on this one also!

Trump wants to defund Planned Parenthood, to make abortions harder to get! But the Globalists won't allow that to ever happen!

Trump wants to get as many folks off of government welfare as possible and put them to work as tax-paying citizens! But the Globalist Democrats and Republicans will never allow that to happen.

Trump wants to "Make America Great Again" by returning her to her former glory and power economically, militarily, politically, and spiritually. He wants our nation to return to capitalism and free enterprise which made us economically strong many years ago! He wants to build up our military so we can negotiate with our enemies from a position of strength-- not weakness. He wants to guarantee our freedoms and liberties to worship God, unhindered by a tyrannical government. He wants to get the government out of our churches, not get God out of the public sector. He wants to continue to secure our Second Amendment rights to keep and bear arms. He wants to get us out of debt so that we will never succumb to the dictatorial powers of any foreign enemy nation. All of this sounds so right and natural to the ears of those who know and appreciate our history. All of this is in line with the philosophical ideals of our founding fathers. All of this sounds so wise, frugal, righteous, and even biblical! But the Globalists who REALLY run our country will have none of it! Nearly all the Socialist Democrats and most of the Globalist Republicans are becoming financially wealthy by ensuring the continual destruction of our Republic as we morph into the biblically prophesied One-world Government. They cannot at this juncture relinquish their control of their "Global American Feudal System" to this independent acting President who wasn't supposed to win over their comrade Hillary. They cannot be a willing participant in "Making America Great Again" because it would diminish their political power and quickly reduce the large amounts of cash currently being deposited into their off-shore bank accounts! And they certainly cannot just resign and walk away from their global "Mafia" bosses who own them because they know too much! If they tried to walk away, they would be facing a most certain "accidental" death or a staged "suicide!" So like good little puppets, they will continue to fight The Donald at every turn and collect their cash reward at the end of each day! And they have enough comrades in our nation's government to join them!

John McCain, John Boehner, Paul Ryan, Lindsey Graham, Mitch McConnell, and a slew of other Global Republicans have joined their New World Order comrades on the other side of the political aisle to make certain that none of the policies, laws, and court rulings of their Global Puppeteers that have been in place for the past 80 years will be reversed by this rogue and "arrogant" President. He's clearly not one of them. And he's clearly not on board with their evil plan to not only kill America-- but to bury Her!

Charles Krauthammer is a syndicated columnist and journalist who was anything BUT a Trump fan. When the Donald was running for office, Charles spared no words in his disdain for this Presidential hopeful. But after Trump's first year in office, and as of the writing of this book, "Charles the Criticizer" became "Charles the Admirer" with this new assessment of Donald Trump:

"Trump is not a liberal or a conservative. He's a "Pragmatist". (Definition: A pragmatist is someone who is practical and focused on reaching a goal. A pragmatist usually has a straightforward, matter-of-fact approach and doesn't let emotions distract him or her.). Trump doesn't see a problem as "liberal" or "conservative!" He sees a problem and understands that it must be fixed. That is a quality that should be admired and applauded, not condemned!

Viewing problems from a liberal perspective has resulted in the creation of more problems, more entitlement programs, more victims, more government, more political correctness, and more attacks on the working class in all economic strata. Viewing things according to the so-called Republican conservative perspective has brought continued spending and globalism to the detriment of American interest and wellbeing as well as denial of what the real problems are: weak, ineffective, milquetoast leadership that amounts to "Barney Fife, Deputy Sheriff" oriented appeasement, and afraid of its own shadow. In brief, it has brought liberal ideology with a pachyderm as a mascot juxtaposed to the ass of the Democrat Party.

Immigration isn't a Republican problem, and it isn't a Liberal problem. It is a problem that threatens the very fabric and infrastructure of America. It demands a pragmatic approach, not an approach that is intended to appease one group or the other.

The impending collapse of the economy wasn't a Liberal or Conservative problem. It was and still is an American problem.

That said, until it is viewed as a problem that demands a common-sense approach to resolution, it will never be fixed because the Democrats and Republicans know only one way to fix things, and the longevity of their impracticality has proven to have no lasting effect.

Successful businessmen like Donald Trump find ways to make things work; they do not promise to accommodate. Trump uniquely understand that China's manipulation of currency is not a Republican problem or a Democrat problem. It is a problem that threatens our financial stability, and he understand the proper balance needed to fix it. Here again, successful businessmen like Trump who have weathered the changing tides of economic reality understand what is necessary to make business work, and they, unlike both sides of the political aisle, know that if something doesn't work, you don't continue trying to make it work hoping that at some point it will.

As a pragmatist, Donald Trump hasn't made wild pie-in-the-sky promises of a cell phone in every pocket, free college tuition and a $15 an hour minimum wage for working the drive-through at Carl's Hamburgers. I argue that America needs pragmatists because pragmatists see a problem and find ways to fix them. They do not see a problem and compound it by creating more problems. You may not like Donald Trump, but I suspect that the reason some people do not like him is because:

1) He is antithetical to the 'good old boy' method of brokering backroom deals that fatten the coffers of politicians.
2) They are unaccustomed to hearing a President speak who is unencumbered by the financial shackles of those he owes vis-a-vis donations.

3) He is someone who is free of idiomatic political ideology.
4) He says what he is thinking; unapologetic for his outspoken thoughts; speaks very straightforward using everyday language that can be understood by all (and is offensive to some who dislike him anyway), making him a great communicator, for the most part, who does what he says he will do and:
5) He is someone who understands that it takes more than hollow promises and political correctness to make American great again.

Listening to Hillary Clinton and Bernie Sanders talk about fixing America is like listening to two lunatics trying to 'out crazy' one another. Jeb Bush, John Kasich and Marco Rubio (All Republicans) are owned lock, stock, and barrel by the bankers, corporations, and big dollar donors funding their campaigns (the family of 64 – the New World Order). Bush can deny it, but common sense tells anyone willing to face facts that people don't give tens of millions without expecting something in return.

We have had Democrat and Republican ideologues, and what has it brought us? Are we better off today or worse off? Has it happened overnight, or has it been a steady decline brought on by both parties? I submit that a pragmatist is just what American needs right now. People are quick to confuse and despise confidence as arrogance, but that is common among those who have never accomplished anything in their lives; or politicians who never really solved a problem, because it's better to still have an "issue to be solved, so re-elect me to solve it" (which never happens) and those who have always played it safe (again, all politicians), not willing to risk failure, to try and achieve success.

Donald Trump put his total financial empire at risk in running for President and certainly did not need or possibly even want the job: that says it all. He wants success for this U. S. and her citizens because he loves his country!"

11
The Great Deception Called "The Republican Party"

Anyone who does their homework and is honest in their investigations will conclude that most politicians in the Democratic Party are socialist puppets of the New World Order Globalists. But what most evangelical Christian conservatives don't know is that many (if not most) politicians in the Republican Party on the federal and state levels are willing participants as well in the plan of the NWO to destroy this Republic! The political demarcation line has not only been blurred but erased between these "opposing Parties" which at one time had such clear and vastly distinct philosophical differences for the direction of our country. Now-- only semantics and theatrics separate the two!

In our recent Republican presidential primary debates, there were 17 hopeful candidates on stage, each trying to convince Americans that they were the best choice to lead our country. As far as my research can tell, only Ben Carson, Mike Huckabee, and Donald Trump had no association with the New World Order. The other 14 Republicans were puppets of the Globalists.

Nearly every sitting Republican Senator and many Republican Representatives are members of one or more of the subsidiary Secret Societies of the New World Order, taking their instructions of how to vote on "resolutions" and "bills" from the family of

64! But this just didn't happen overnight! Here's one example of a married couple who supposedly "served" our country as "conservative" Senators years ago: Bob and Elizabeth Dole!

Elizabeth Dole served in three Republican presidential administrations-- Nixon, Reagan, and George H. W. Bush. Before that, she was a registered Democrat. Her resume in the GOP is incredibly diverse:

Commissioner of the Federal Trade Commission
Director of the Office of Public Liaison
U.S. Secretary of Transportation
U.S. Secretary of Labor
Chair of the National Republican Senatorial Committee
Director of the American Red Cross (subsidiary of the NWO)
United States Senator from North Carolina
Mrs. Dole represented herself throughout her political career as a "Christian conservative," securing the support of the

evangelical Christian community. She served under the Globalist puppet Nixon as a registered Democrat before she served under two more puppet Presidents who were also owned by the Globalists. She graduated from Duke and was "groomed" at Harvard-- two schools owned and operated by the family of 64. My research has confirmed that she was one of many "conservative" puppets of the Globalists. Several decades ago, I chatted with a close friend in Washington who worked under Mrs. Dole when she was the Director of the Red Cross. He confirmed my suspicions that she is not who she postulates herself to be. Elizabeth Dole is married to another puppet-- ex-Senator Bob Dole.

Representing Kansas, Bob was the Republican leader of the United States Senate from 1985 to 1996. His career in Congress began in 1961. He was the GOP's vice-presidential nominee in the 1976 elections. And was the Republican presidential nominee in 1996. A short peek at his resume:

Member of the U.S. House
Member of the U.S. Senate
Chair of the Republican National Committee
Head of the Senate Agricultural Committee
Chair of the Senate Finance Committee
Senate Majority Leader

Republican puppet Gerald Ford was told by the Globalists to select Dole to be his running mate in the 1976 election. Bob Dole is a Free Mason, a member of the Russell Lodge No. 177, in Russell, Kansas. He was elevated to the 33rd degree of the Scottish Rite in 1975! (You aren't promoted to the 33rd degree unless you prove to be a faithful and loyal advocate of the New World Order). Presidential candidate Bob Dole and his running mate "conservative" Jack Kemp (1996 elections) were both members of the Bohemian Grove.

These are just two examples of Republicans groomed and educated by the Globalists who portrayed themselves as "conservatives." There are hundreds more. Consider this short list of Republican leaders who were active members of the Bohemian Grove:

George Bush
Gerald Ford
Henry Kissinger
Richard Nixon
Dick Cheney
Alan Greenspan (the head of the Federal Reserve)
Alexander Haig (former Defense Secretary)
Casper Weinberger (former Secretary of State)
George Shultz (former Secretary of State)

Many ex-Presidents have been photographed at these satanically inspired ritualistic meetings (including Ronald

Reagan). The Bohemian Grove members meet at the time when the sun (Aton) is at its highest point of the year- at the summer solstice- June 21st. The summer solstice was adopted by Hitler and his Nazis as their most important day of satanic ritual and celebration. It was the most sacred day on the Nazi calendar.

At the Grove, these leaders of our government participate in necromancy (communicating with the dead), pedophilia, sacrificing children and animals in the fire, and the worshipping of the demon owl-god called "Moloch" (the same demon-god in the Bible to whom the Hebrews, Babylonians, Egyptians, Canaanites, Phoenicians and Carthaginians sacrificed their children in the fire). The false demon-god "Baal" in the Bible is referred to as "the god of the groves." The Grove members also worship the same demonic "sun god" as do the Muslims (Allah).

I watched George Bush Jr. when he had his exit interview on TV after serving as President for eight years. Brian Williams asked him if he believed that the God of the Bible was exactly the same God that the Muslims worship (Allah). Without hesitation, George replied, "Yes! I believe that the God of the Christians and the God of the Muslims are one and the same God!" George Bush had secured the conservative votes of millions of unsuspecting "Christians" in two national elections, while continuing to worship his false demon sun-god and owl-god at the Grove meetings. While in office, Bush peppered several of his speeches with the words: "New World Order."

We are not talking about a few in the Republican Party who participate in these despicable events. Many leaders in our nation who legislate our laws and dictate our lives are acting members of satanic secret societies. It is estimated that nearly

85 percent of the Bohemian Grove members are originally from California (that explains a lot, doesn't it?).

Has anyone even noticed that the stars in the Republican Party Logo have been turned upside down since the year 2000? Many satanic societies have notoriously used stars in their logos. No big deal! Right? But did you know that one of the many demonic gods mentioned in the Bible is a "star-god?" These "heavenly hosts" were even being worshipped by God's special nation, Israel. And after several warnings through His prophets, God had to step in and punish them severely for their demon-worship atrocities. (Jeremiah 19:13). They were building shrines and obelisks (like the Washington Monument) and idols on every high hill and under every green tree (like the Bohemian Grove). There was sexual perversion (homosexuality and pedophilia), and God's people became as depraved as the heathen nations surrounding them. (I Kings 14: 23-24).

Turning the stars on the elephant emblem upside down is no accident, and certainly no printing mistake (as they would have us believe). If you notice, the upside-down stars resemble the head of a goat, with its horns pointing upward and its long face pointing downward. The goat head is a symbol of all satan worshippers! And there are many of them in the Republican Party.

Astrology is forbidden by God in the Bible. In fact, going to any other source besides the One True God for knowledge, information, and power is called "witchcraft and sorcery!" To worship the Bohemian Grove Owl-god of knowledge is witchcraft and sorcery. To worship the Muslim sun-god "Allah" is witchcraft and sorcery! To look to the demonic star-gods of Astrology is witchcraft and sorcery. But our Presidents and Senators don't care what God has to say about these things. They have been duped by the demon powers working through their "mafia bosses" in the New World Order. They have sold their souls to the devil in exchange for money and power! (Even Eleanor Roosevelt, Nancy Reagan, and Hillary Clinton practiced the demonic craft of astrology in the White House).

Many decades ago, the Republican Party joined the Democratic Party in caving to the dark and destructive agenda of the New World Order. Our Republic was destroyed! Our Democracy was demolished! What remains is a gargantuan global government of totalitarianism! Whether it's Franklin and Eleanor, Bob and Elizabeth, Jimmy and Rosalynn, Bill and Hillary, George and Laura, or Barack and Michelle ("Michael"), they all serve the "ascended masters" of the spirit-world and the political masters of the New World Order!

12
The Death of America through Mergers & Acquisitions

The Republic of the United States of America has died. She wasn't killed by an enemy military invasion. No army tanks or ground troops were needed to destroy her. No Stealth Bombers or MiG Fighter Jets were used for her destruction. Not even a nuclear warhead was used to wipe her out. She was killed by her own government! A government that didn't even need to confiscate her guns! It wasn't necessary!

She was neutralized by those who used her own system of democracy to turn against her. She didn't even resist! There was no struggle whatsoever! No fight! She willingly gave up and died. The only thing left for her is the funeral and the burial.

Many decades ago, the Globalists instructed their puppets Presidents Woodrow Wilson, Franklin D. Roosevelt, Dwight D. Eisenhower, and Richard M. Nixon to begin the process of accomplishing three things that would in effect kill our independent, sovereign nation:

1.)   Create the Federal Reserve Act with a Board that would be run by the 64-family Elitists who would set our interest rates on loans and control the economy of our entire nation. From this point on, a few families of foreigners working through the Fed Board would dictate the fluctuation of our economy at their pleasure and orchestrate the death of our Republic. The puppet Presidents would select the board members including the Chairman to make the appearance to the public that this is a government run agency, when in fact, it is a New World Order agency completely manipulating our entire economy to fulfill their plans and to fill their coffers!

2.) Continue working toward developing an organization independent of government control and restraints that will indefinitely enforce the mandated taxes of the NWO through our own government. This was strengthened under Eisenhower and given even more power under President Clinton's administration. The Internal Revenue Service has bloated to an unprecedented annual budget of 11.7 billion dollars and approximately 100,000 employees today. All under the control of the Globalists.

3.) Work toward the process of removing gold as the foundational standard that gave value to our paper money. Their puppet President Richard Nixon finalized their plan to take us off the gold standard and make our paper money of no value! They deemed this to be a necessary action in order to fulfill their agenda to make ours a "cashless society" and to usher in their new system of people control with their permanent micro-chip.

Their plan to remove our personal control over our hard-earned money and our own decisions of how we would invest that money worked precisely in the manner and time which they had hope! They destroyed our economic way of life, our freedom to do with our money what we wanted and took control over our nation's entire monetary system; fundamentally changing our common citizen-run sovereign Republic to a corporation owned and ruled by them. They actually believe they are being kind, merciful, gracious and philanthropical by "allowing" us to keep a small percentage of our salaries after we pay them nearly half of what we earn in yearly taxes. They are in control of our money-- not us! And we allowed them to do this without any resistance!

I remember back in the decades of the eighties and nineties when the huge mergers of corporations began. I noticed the bank mergers first. The North Carolina National Bank (NCNB) merged with what soon became Nation's Bank. This bank was bought by Bank of America. This huge bank quickly, and I mean QUICKLY became the 2nd largest bank in the United States, close behind JPMorgan Chase. It seemed like overnight that Bank of America and Wells Fargo Bank (the 3rd largest US bank) bought out most of the banks in our country. And when you follow the money trail of the mergers, buy-outs, and hostile takeovers by these two banks whose major shareholders are overseas foreigners, all roads lead to the City Bank of London, (currently the Bank of England), owned and operated by the Rothschilds, one of the central families in the Cabal of 64! The Rothchild family are also major shareholders of the Federal Reserve Bank of New York. In just a few decades, these financial mergers and acquisitions put most of the world's invested wealth into the hands of a few people. "He who has the gold rules!" And there was no resistance on the part of the American people!

The Rockefellers have always owned and managed oil companies! But in the decade of the eighties, they brilliantly manipulated major mergers that fully secured for them most of the world's crude oil fields, including those in China. They cornered the market on oil in our country by using their puppet organization- the EPA- to effectively shut down America's oil fields and off shore drilling operations so they could be the sole owners and controllers of the world's oil supply. They also effectively used their EPA puppets of our government to close down nearly all of our coal mines and coal plants, convincing all unsuspecting Americans that it was for our good. Their ruse was that without those nasty polluted coal mines, coal plants and oil fields, we can now have much cleaner air, water, and soil-- leading us to "a better quality of life." In reality, the Rockefellers were the architects behind the plan to transition our nation from oil and coal to nuclear power! Why? Well it certainly wasn't because nuclear power was "safer and cleaner" as they proposed and propagated. It was because their global "partners in crime"- the Duke family- owned most of the nuclear power plants. Whether it was through oil, coal, or nuclear power-- these New World Order families were successful in getting us to become totally dependent on them! They continue this day to use oil and nuclear power as their leveraging tools to force nations to submit to them. They know that oil is the lifeblood of every industrial nation. Without it-- the nation dies! So our governmental "Representatives" continue to fill the money coffers of their Bosses (the Rockefellers, Dukes and Rothschilds) with billions, without ever questioning their motives or actions. The citizens of this country believed their lies that it would benefit all Americans. So they acquiesced with no fight!

In the eighties, I noticed the major airline corporate mergers. US Air bought out several airlines, and other large airlines bought out many smaller ones. Now, the principle owner of these merged airlines are foreigners-- not citizens of the United States. Our travel is now controlled by these few Elitists families. They can (and will) eventually shut it down at their good pleasure-- with the deceptive guise that it is for "our own safety and protection." The citizens of this country stood by without a fight and allowed it all to happen, believing their lies that it was all for the best!

Our own government leaders in Congress drove up our federal deficit to over 18 trillion dollars. Our nation cannot even pay the interest on our debts. So Congress borrowed more money from China, driving our debts upward still! This was all accomplished by the design of the Globalists in charge. To weaken a nation, destroy its economic infrastructure first by orchestrating lavish out-of-control spending and driving it into major debt. Kill the economy-- kill the whole nation! And the citizens stood by and believed their lies that this was for our good. No fight!

In the late seventies and early eighties, our government continued to raise the corporate taxes to the point that most of our major industries began to move overseas. Our steel industries closed down and moved! Our textile industries folded and relocated! Our auto industries were sold to foreigners and relocated out of the country. Nearly every significant corporation in America moved to Mexico, moved across the Atlantic to Europe, or ceased operations indefinitely. This happened so quickly that when Americans finally noticed, we were no longer manufacturing anything of significance anymore. Millions lost their jobs! Millions filed for bankruptcy. When we combine all this with the financially foolish and easily obtainable government housing loans (Fannie Mae and Freddie Mac) and the student college loans which defaulted and the non-sensible free money in the billions our government was giving away to foreign countries who were our sworn enemies, it becomes blatantly obvious that something has gone awry! These actions of default and "generosity" make no sense whatsoever, unless you understand that they were done by design to bankrupt this nation and force it to willingly submit to the One-world Government with a global citizenship.

The Global government has been in control of our nation for many decades. Their goal has always been to destroy our nation economically, politically, militarily, and socially. Every single thing that I have mentioned has been by design. These are not just random mishaps! These are not just foolish blunders by our own government. They WANTED to financially bankrupt America. They WANTED to fundamentally change our culture by continuing to allow illegal immigrants to cross our borders and vote in our elections. They WANT the traditional, biblical family unit destroyed. That's why they fund the sexually perverted LGBT community and fund the sitcoms on TV that portray homosexuality as a "normal, healthy lifestyle," and in a sitcom with a traditional marriage portray the wife as being very emotionally and intellectually strong and the husband as being clueless ("Everybody Loves Raymond"). They WANT the rioters in the streets destroying property, demolishing historical statues, dressing up like vaginas, and killing cops. They WANT millions of babies killed in the womb each year. They WANT Americans deceived in their thinking that we have free elections. They WANT us to continue to have the illusion of freedom of speech and the illusion of personal property ownership, when in reality we own nothing. They own it all! They WANT to fuel the fire of hate and cause division by pitting one race and ethnic group against the other. This is their designed plan to create chaos, disorder, and anarchy in this last bastion of freedom called America. They had to create "disorder" to bring in their "new order!" They know that it's over for our Republic. They laugh when they view us going to the polls to vote; knowing full well that both candidates are owned and controlled by them. They don't care which one we vote into office!

It's over! It will never be reversed! There is no more semblance of our once great Republic! No one lone President can presently reverse everything that the Globalists had installed years ago. It was said by many attorneys that Obamacare was legally set up so that it could never be dismantled, deleted, disregarded, discarded, or destroyed. It was put into place by the careful design of the Globalist for "people control!" Universal Healthcare was crafted as the first step to control the masses with the goal in mind of the eventual introduction and the inevitable installation of the micro-chip, which will be inserted into the hand or forehead of every "useful idiot." The New World Order Socialists had to first install Universal Healthcare to make the micro-chip much more palatable to the deceived, vulnerable, and cooperative "serfs!" The chip (like everything else) will be introduced as a "good" thing:

"It's for your protection," they will say!
"It's in case your child is lost or is kidnapped," they will say!
"It's in case your grandfather wanders off and gets lost," they will say!
"It's there so you can buy food to feed your family," they will say!

"It's so that all your medical history and insurance info is available in the unlikely event you have a car wreck or a heart attack," they will say!
"It's to make it easier for you to do your banking and all your financial transactions," they will say!

And most gullible Americans will take the bait (chip) that leads down the slippery slope to the pre-designed trap of the slavery of global citizenship! The implanted micro-chip will be presented as a "voluntary" thing at first. But soon will be forced upon all the global citizen slaves of the New World Order dictatorship!

13
The Kingdom of God Vs
The New World Order

Was America ever a "nation under God?" Was she ever a "Christian nation?" Or was she just an experiment by members of several satanic, secret societies across the pond in Europe. Check this out:

"In Europe, occult leaders were told by their familiar spirits (demons) centuries ago that the new American continent was to be established as the new 'Atlantis', and its destiny was to assume the leadership of the drive to the New World Order. The United States of America was chosen to lead the world into this kingdom of antichrist from the beginning.

Since 1776, our leadership (U.S. government) has been consistently moving us toward the luciferian 'New World Order!' This leadership has always been working through Secret Societies, misleading us as to their true intentions.

This is why our study today is so critical: it demonstrates beyond a shadow of a doubt that our leadership has knowingly and consistently been pursuing a hidden agenda which, when fully carried out, will mean the destruction of our nation (the U.S.) as we know it today and the beginning of the biblical Great Tribulation. Our leaders are currently and consistently calling this system the New World Order'!" (Free Masonry).

When our forefathers were finished with their endeavors to create their new "experiment" of a government "of the people, for the people, and by the people," and when their documents were all voted on and signed, Benjamin Franklin came out of the last meeting and was quickly approached by a curious bystander awaiting the results:

"Mr. Franklin, what form of government do we have?"
To which Franklin replied, "A Republic, sir, if you can keep it!"

Well, Mr. Franklin, if we ever truly had it, we obviously didn't keep it! It slipped out of our hands like the rapidly falling sand in an hour glass! The word "keep" in the Hebrew language means "to guard!" And we failed to guard possibly the best form of government (short of a theocracy) in the history of mankind! But here's the good news: Whether we were snookered from the very beginning, or whether we had a Republic then lost it, none of this took God by surprise! In fact, it all fits into His eternal Kingdom plans to judge this wicked nation and the entire world for their rebellion against Him!

Because the Bible is the Word of God, every single prophecy to date has been fulfilled in an incredibly accurate manner. Everything God told His prophets centuries ago concerning Israel has today transpired exactly as God said it would-- to the exact time and place! And God even told us about what would happen in the "last days" right before His Son Jesus returns to set up His eternal Kingdom on this earth.

1.)   Many centuries ago, God said that in the last days Israel would become a sovereign nation again. This happened in 1948.

2.)   God said that Jerusalem would again be in the hands of the Jews. This occurred in 1967.

3.)   God said that in the last days Jerusalem would be the capitol of Israel again. This happened as of the writing of this book under President Trump (2018).

4.)   God told us that near the end, the eyes of all governments would be on Jerusalem. That the temple would be rebuilt. That there would be a false "peace treaty" brokered and signed by the ant-christ, then broken by him. The final specifics for that treaty are being negotiated and hammered out right now with Trump's son-n-law, Jared Kushner as the chief facilitator and negotiator.

5.)   God said that there would be a world dictator who would be possessed and empowered by satan himself.

God said there would be a One-world government out of which would come an arrogant evil ruler who would stop at nothing in exercising and asserting his power over every nation on the earth. This ruler would broker a contractual agreement (covenant) between Israel and her Arab enemies (Muslims) that would allow Israel to rebuild her temple and resume her religious ceremonies (which include animal sacrifices to Yahweh)-- in exchange for Israel's submission to the New World Order. This "treaty of peace and unity" will be viewed by the world as the ultimate deal that will propel the world leader to become a hero to the Jews, the Muslims, the "Christians" (the Roman Catholic Church and the World Council of Churches), and the rest of the religious and political world. But he will break his promises and his treaty with Israel in the short span of three and one-half years, setting up an image of himself in the newly built Jewish temple and requiring all Jews to worship him... or die!

The present Prime Minister of Israel is Benjamin Netanyahu, a conservative who seems currently to be a proponent of national sovereignty. Many of his speeches are peppered with his obvious disdain for the Socialist Globalists. He knows who they are and wants nothing to do with them or their sinister plans to bring Israel to her knees. So if we are close to the end of the "last days," Netanyahu will either cave to the wishes of the Globalists, succumbing to their irresistible "bone" of the much-coveted Jewish temple, or he will be taken out of the way (neutralized). We shall see!

The Republic of the United States of America has died (if it ever existed). The sovereign governments of every nation on earth have died-- except for Israel. This tiny nation that is near and dear to the heart of God will never die. They have recently discovered enough oil in their deserts that they need not ever be "leveraged," coerced, or defeated by the New World Order. But they will be temporarily hoodwinked by the world leader (anti-christ) who will offer to them the tantalizing "bone" they have always craved: their third temple!

It is clear that satan, along with his entire kingdom of darkness is behind the New World Order, working through secret societies and government leaders. Ever since as "Lucifer" he garnished a rebellion with one-third of the angels (now working with the demons) and unsuccessfully attempted to usurp the authority of God (which got his wicked butt thrown out of Heaven), and ever since his interrupted and squashed attempt to unify and control the world at the Tower of Babel (the city of Babylon), satan has been on an unending and relentless quest to rule the world. His bid to rule the universe from Heaven was thwarted by God and he was cast down to the earth, where he now bids to rule the world through the cooperation of the government of the United States of America. The One-world Government of the New World Order is the agency through which he will give it one more try.

Through his World Government, and by his World Leader (the anti-christ), satan will have uninterrupted political, economic, and religious control of the earth for only seven years. Then he, his demons (including the ones Hillary consorted with), his human political leaders, and everyone else in the New World Order system will be cast by God into the Lake of Fire. The true King, Master, and Lord of the universe will then rule and reign; restoring righteousness, justice, and peace on the earth! No more Secret Societies. No more Free Masons. No more Illuminati. No more Bohemian Grove. No more Skull and Bones. No more false religions. No more illusions of freedom and democracy. No more pretentious Republics. No more ACLU! No more LGBT! No more pretend "conservative" Republicans. No more liberal socialistic Democrats! No more tyrannical dictatorships. Only the purest form of a theocratic government-- a monarchy... under the powerful and authoritative and absolute rule of King Jesus! (Isaiah 9:6). Centuries ago, God told His prophet Daniel what would transpire during the "last days"-- describing the Great Tribulation Period when the One-world government is temporarily in control:

"Toward the end of their kingdoms (world empires), when the governments of the earth have become morally rotten (the USA), an angry king shall rise to power (anti-christ from the NWO) with great shrewdness (deception) and intelligence. His power shall be mighty (tyrannical), but it shall be satanic strength and not his own (satan himself will possess this man). Prospering wherever he turns, he will destroy all who oppose him, though their armies be mighty; and he will devastate God's people (he will persecute Jews and Christians). He will be a master of deception, defeating many by catching them off guard (at first he will appear to be compassionate, loving, and kind-- like Hitler before he was elected), as they bask in false security (false peace, false unity). Without warning, he will destroy those who oppose him (including the "useful idiots" who brought him to power). So great will he fancy himself to be, that he will even attempt to take on the Prince of Peace in battle (he will attempt to defeat Jesus and His heavenly armies at the battle of Armageddon). But in doing so, he will seal his own doom, for he shall be broken by the hand of God (Jesus is the "hand of God" who will defeat the anti-christ in the Valley of Megiddo upon His return). Though no human means could overpower this evil dictator, God will destroy him!" (Daniel 8:23-25; TLB).

In the history of the world, there have been many men whom satan's demon spirits have possessed which led them on a quest to rule the world. The "spirit guides" (ascended masters) which controlled them also empowered them and persuaded them to kill millions of their enemies and even their own people. They "sacrificed the few for the good of the many":

Nimrod
King Nebuchadnezzar
King Sennacherib
King Saul
King Caesar
Nero of Rome
Alexander the Great
Napoleon
King Henry
Joseph Stalin (killed 20 million people)
Krushev
Brezhnev
Mussolini
Hitler (killed 13 million)
Mao Tse-Tung (killed 45 million)
Ho Chi Minh (his name means "the Enlightener")
Pol Pot (killed two million)

These men (and others like them) were bent on world domination. Satan had convinced them (and they had deceitfully convinced themselves) that they had a legitimate shot at ruling the entire earth. But it wasn't God's timing. It wasn't on God's "end-time" calendar. Just like satan when he attempted to set up his own government in Heaven, they each failed miserably! But the next world leader will not fail. He will be successful for nearly seven years! The first three and one-half years of his rule will go somewhat smoothly. But the second half of his dictatorship will make all these other evil tyrants look like Sunday school teachers!

14

How Should We Then Live?

Now that we know more about how our government has been operating for the past 80+ years, and we know biblically what will transpire in the near future under a tyrannical one-world government, what should we Christians do? How should we live?

Many followers of Christ have joined their local militias, thinking they have a chance to fight against the strong military of the New World Order and turn this thing around. They defend their thinking by recalling how the early American colonists composed of farmers, militiamen, and a ragtime army fought against the world's greatest army and navy (Great Britain) and defeated them to secure our independence. They look forward to the opportunity to repeat history by defending with honor the American flag and the Republic it represents. There's only one problem-- there is no more Republic to defend! There's not even a remnant left. It died years ago! Don't get me wrong, I understand the passion, bravery, and patriotism of these true American militias. But their plans to stockpile weapons and ammo to fight against a global military will be met with futility... and death! Their patriotism is commendable; but their plan lacks wisdom and discernment!

Some followers of Christ have for years lived off the grid, no longer dependent on the government for electricity, water, sewage, food, health insurance, social security, etc. The Amish community on American soil have for over a century been prepared to face the inevitable arrival of the biblical Tribulation Period when the evil anti-christ comes to power. They know what's coming down the pipe, so in each generation the parents have taught their children how to live in a self - sufficient environment by growing their own food, digging their own wells, building their own windmills and watermills, building their own homes, cutting firewood for heat and cooking; and hunting, trapping, and fishing for meat! They and others who have learned survival techniques will be the least affected when all hell breaks loose on this earth. But this does not at all mean that they will go unscathed by the terrors of the evil dictator!

Here's a few simple but wise things that some have suggested we begin to do in preparation for "that great and terrible day" described in the Book of Revelation:

1.) Get out of debt! Sell that extra car. Downsize from that huge, expensive house! Sell everything you don't need. Owe no man anything! Live debt-free!

2.) Learn how to grow your own food and learn how to preserve what you grow! Take the cash you have from selling the unnecessary things and buy nonperishable foods (freeze-dried and canned).

3.) Find an abundant natural water source nearby. You may have to boil the water to make it drinkable, but at least you'll have it available. You can survive 40 days without food, but you can't survive 3 days without water.

4.) Have a heat source for the winters (plenty of firewood).

5.) Whatever you do, when the implanted micro-chip is introduced, avoid it at all costs. This could possibly be the "mark of the beast" described in the Book of Revelation. Avoid anything permanent that the government wants to put on your body or in your body. I believe the Bible is clear that the true followers of Christ will not accept this "mark!" Only those who are deceived by the satanic New World Order will gladly receive this government sanctioned mark or chip! The moment you receive this mark or chip-- they own you! They control you!

Many Bible scholars believe that the United States of America is the wicked "Babylon" described in Revelation. If that is the case, America will be destroyed in one day-- probably by nukes! Just as the twin towers in New York were brought down in a matter of minutes, every major city in this nation will be quickly destroyed.

Some believe that we Christians might possibly go through a portion of the seven year "Tribulation Period" when God pours out His wrath upon this wicked nation and upon all the earth. Some scholars think we will be "raptured" out of here before the anti-christ comes into power and the New World Order is fully installed. God has had a plan in place for this world long before He created anything. He knows exactly what He is doing in all the governments and in each individual life! Nothing takes Him by surprise. Nothing moves Him to fear! Nothing induces worry or anxiety in Him! If you truly belong to Him, you need not stress or worry or fear either! He will take care of you! Trust Him with your very life! In these troubled times, don't trust your government. Don't trust your neighbors. Don't trust the religious leaders of your denomination. Don't trust the soon to be introduced world leader. Don't even trust your best friend! Listen to what God says to you:

"Cursed is the man who puts his trust in mortal man and turns his heart away from

God. This man is like a stunted shrub in the desert, with no hope for the future; he lives in the barren wilderness (confusion); good times pass him by forever (it's over for him). But blessed is the man who trusts in the Lord and has made the Lord his hope and confidence. No matter what happens to him, (no matter how bad the world gets), he will remain unshaken." (Jeremiah 17:5-8).

Even though we are to "render unto Caesar that which is Caesar's" by paying our taxes, God in His Word forbids followers of Jesus to take any secret oaths or to pledge our allegiance to any form of human government (Jeremiah 5:7; II Chronicles 36:13; Matthew 5:33-37; John 18:20; Proverbs 22:26). The pagan satanic religions of the Illuminati, Free Masonry, and the Bohemian Grove require of their members the verbalizing of secret oaths (curses) and allegiance. When one reaches the 32nd degree in the Masons, they are instructed to pledge their allegiance to Allah-- the demonic sun god (which is why President Bush- himself a Mason- believes that the God of the Bible and the god of the Muslims are one and the same. He will discover the truth very soon). Many true believers in Jesus continue to pledge their allegiance to the flag that represents this evil, wicked nation-- even though it is obvious to them that our nation is no longer "One nation, under God, indivisible, with liberty and justice for all." We have become "One nation, owned by the New World Order, under satan, divisible, with feudal slavery and injustice for all!" If you, as a child of God continue pledging your allegiance to this wicked, satan-controlled nation, (or to the soon coming world leader), you will be held accountable by the Most-High God!

The United States of America is not the Kingdom of God! It never has been, and it never will be! God tells us that as Christians, we are not citizens of this earth. Our citizenship is in Heaven. (Philippians

3:20; Ephesians 2:6; Colossians 3:1). As such, we are instructed by Jesus to "seek first the Kingdom of God and His righteousness." (Matthew 6:33). We are to be loyal and faithful servants to the One True God-- Jesus! Not feudal slaves of the New World Order! Not servants of the demon-god "Allah!" And certainly not willing subjects and accomplices of the anti-christ!

The Bible is clear that many Christians will die a martyr's death at the hands of this ruthless "end-time" world leader. But their rewards in Heaven will be worth it all. (And I'm not talking about 70 virgins; but the smile on the face of their Redeemer and Friend-- Jesus).

In the meantime, how should followers of Jesus get involved in politics? To what extent should we participate in the obviously rigged and flawed process of voting those we consider honest and honorable into office?

We must understand that decades ago the Globalist family of 64 manipulated and rigged the entire process of our elections to the point where not just anyone can run for office on the state and federal level. One must be a millionaire already before entering the arena of becoming a viable and electable candidate. The Political Action Committees (PAC) were created by the New World Order to ensure that only their handpicked candidates in both political parties would be facing each other on the ballot. It now takes millions of dollars to run for Governor on the state level and even more money to run for US Congress or the office of President. They rigged it so that the common American citizen can no longer run for public office. And only multi-millionaires can run as an "independent." But their own puppets who were educated by them and funded with their PAC money will be the only electable candidates strategically placed on the final ballot.

For nearly a century, the Globalists have brilliantly manipulated our entire election process to ensure that only their candidates would win. But in their semi successful plans to taint all of our elections, they obviously failed to cover all the possible scenarios. They let a self-made billionaire slip through the cracks of their "full-proof" agenda—the Donald! Now, they are scrambling and reorganizing to devise a plan for his demise. But they most certainly will not allow him to reverse or destroy everything they have put in place for the past 80+ years. If Trump gets in the way of their final plans to fully usher in the New World Order, they will remove him either by impeachment (so that it appears to the public as a "legal" and "democratic" process by our own government), or by "neutralization" (global-speak for "assassination").

Should Christians continue to vote? For moral and social issues—a resounding YES! For candidates on the local level— YES! For candidates on the national level, I am not so sure that it matters anymore. For many years we have been voting for "the lesser of two evils." But voting for the "lesser of two evils" is still voting for evil. Whether it be the liberals voting for their favorite Marxist-socialist candidates, or conservatives voting for their "snake in the grass" Republican candidates, they are all supporting those candidates who have themselves sold out to the One-world government... and have sold us out as well. All voters would be voting for the New World Order system of the anti-christ!

I leave you with this counsel and instruction if, when, or how you vote: Pray first! Seek God's counsel. You can't go wrong when He speaks to you and instructs you in each of your decisions— including politics!

How should we then live? Remember, God tells us in His Word that we are not fighting against people, nor are we fighting against governments like the New World Order

(Ephesians 6:12-13). Our warfare is a spiritual one, not a physical or political one. All that is happening right now in our nation and in the entire world was already foretold by God centuries ago. God said it must happen before the return of Jesus. And we cannot stop it! But we can pray for wisdom in how we are to respond to it, and how we are to prepare for it!

Epilogue

The design to kill America was relatively quite simple and easy for the family of 64:

1.)   They infiltrated all three branches of our government with their groomed and educated puppets as their willing accomplices. They then instructed these puppets how to vote on every law and how to rule in every courtroom case; effectively removing all power from the common people. They filled the bank accounts of their puppets with millions as their reward for their loyalty.

2.) They invested some money in our economy, loaned our nation money with high interest rates, got our corporations and banks healthy, got our economy strong and prosperous, taxed our citizens and corporations extensively, bolstered our pharmaceutical companies, and got the billions of dollars of cocaine flowing into our nation.

3.) They used our system of free enterprise and capitalism to make $trillions$ for themselves. Then destroyed the very system that increased their wealth exponentially by introducing liberal socialism. They propped us up, made their money, then destroyed us.

4.) When they finished using us to make themselves more wealthy, and when they maxed out on their investments and returns, they centralized all of our banks and began the process of dismantling our economic, political, and social infrastructure through driving up the national debt to the point that we can't pay the interest, increased the welfare rolls, made health insurance unaffordable, made Obamacare mandatory, gave financial rewards to all the illegal immigrants that came across our borders, etc., etc.

5.) Through their puppet Presidents Clinton and Obama, they drastically weakened our military with massive budget cuts and by spreading our soldiers all over the globe. In essence, making us defenseless.

As of 2014, 6.3 trillion dollars of our U.S. debt is owned by foreign investors such as Japan, China, Belgium, Caribbean Banking, Oil exporters (Rockefellers), Brazil, Switzerland, Taiwan, the U.K., Hong Kong, Vietnam, etc. This 6.3 figure is 45 percent of our debt. The largest "private" institution which has loaned money to the U.S. government is the Federal Reserve (one out of every eight dollars). Nearly all of the money has been lent since 2008. This money is used for "quantitative easing programs" (including entitlement programs) to avoid a "recession." There has never been an audit or Congressional investigation for this entire program. There is no accountability... and the Globalists want it that way! How did we become such a substantial borrower of the Fed's funds?

First, the unelected governors of the unconstitutional central banks have an absolute stranglehold and monopoly over the flow of our nation's money and credit. Not since its inception in 1913 has there ever been a thorough audit or an accounting to Congress about the Fed's activities. During its century long reign over the financial "well-being" of our country, the Federal Reserve has manipulated our currency until it is nearly worthless. Meanwhile, the Globalists in our Congress have turned a blind eye and a deaf ear to the crisis and to the calls of the American people to control it.

The fact is that since that day in 1913, the dollar has lost over 95 percent of its purchasing power. Most, if not all of this precipitous decline was caused by the monetary policy of the Federal Reserve. (Stats by Joe Wolverton, J. D. for "The New American").

Approximately 545 people are still in control of over 300 million people in this nation. And 64 global families are still in control of those 545 people!

They have succeeded at every level in their plans to put to death what was left of our dying Republic. And they used our very own government against us as their instrument of death to accomplish their plans. It was all by design. And it all fits into the eschatological narrative of the biblical prophecies of God. What will be the final nail in the coffin? Maybe the micro-chip in the hand or forehead! Who knows?

Conclusion

The Bible declares: "Blessed is the nation whose God is the Lord." (Psalm 33:12). But it also says, "The wicked shall be turned into Hell, along with all the nations that forget God!" (Psalm 9:17).

The "god" of this nation is not the true God of the Scriptures. Christians continue to say, "God bless America," but He can never bless anything that is wicked. And He will never again bless this nation that long ago turned its back on Him to worship other "demon gods."

If you truly belong to God, having confessed your sins to Him; having put our trust in the finished work of Jesus on the cross; having been born-again by the Holy Spirit-- you need not fear the future! Read the prayer of one of God's daughters, praising Him for His future plans for His children on this earth:

"I magnify You, my God, for Your absolute purity, holiness, and justice, as the Judge to whom all people must give account. I praise You that Your fairness is intertwined with everything You do... that when the time is ripe You will end all sin and injustice, all corruption, all immorality... that You will right all wrongs and reward all loving service and suffering for Your sake. Thank You that Your Son will return from Heaven with a shout of triumph, that the

dead in Christ will be raised imperishable...
and in a flash, in the twinkling of an eye, we
shall all be utterly changed. We shall see the
radiance of His face and the glorious
majesty of His power. It will be a breath-
taking wonder and splendor unimaginable
to all who believe. Thank You that whatever
we must go through now is less than
nothing compared with the magnificent
future You have planned for us.

What a joy to know that the government
will finally be on Christ's shoulders, and
that there will be no end to the increase of
His government and peace (Isaiah 9:6)
...that His kingdom will be established with
justice and righteousness (no more evil),
from then on and forevermore. Your
kingdom is an everlasting kingdom... a
kingdom that cannot be shaken. You will
never be voted out; no coup will ever
dethrone You! For all eternity You are the
King of kings and Lord of lords. To You be
all power and authority and glory and

honor and dominion forever and ever!"
(Ruth Myers: "31 Days of Praise").

The Holy Spirit through the Apostle Paul
wrote:

"These troubles and sufferings of ours are,
after all, quite small and won't last very
long. Yet this short time of distress will
result in God's richest blessings upon us
forever and ever (short term pain—long
term pleasures). So we don't focus upon
what we can see happening right now, the
troubles all around us. But we look
forward to the joys in Heaven which we
have not yet seen. The troubles will soon
be over, but the joys to come will last
forever." (II Corinthians 4: 17-18; Romans
8: 18; TLB).

God told King David to write these words:

"O nations of the world, confess that God
alone is glorious and strong. Give Him the
glory He deserves. Worship Him alone. Tell

all the nations that Jehovah-Yahweh reigns. He rules the world. His power can never be overthrown. He will soon judge all nations with His righteous judgements. The Lord is coming to judge the earth. He will judge the world with His righteousness and Truth!" (Psalm 96: 713; TLB).

Consider what God told Jeremiah to record for us what will transpire in the "last days":

"The Lord has a case against all nations, all mankind. He will slaughter all the wicked. The punishment will go from nation to nation. His great whirlwind of wrath shall rise against the farthest corners of the earth. And you will find no place to hide from His wrath. No way to escape! People now living undisturbed (in peace and unity) will be cut down by the fierceness of the anger of the Lord." (Jeremiah 25: 31-36; TLB).

If my grandfather could talk to me from Heaven right now (which is forbidden by God), he would probably say, "Thomas, promise me four things:

Don't ever buy a new American made or foreign made car. The auto industry has become a global one and your money will be funding the evil New World Order who owns all the car manufacturers worldwide. Don't ever, EVER vote for a damned Democrat OR a damned Republican. They have all sold their souls to the satanically inspired One-world government. Don't ever take the micro-chip in your hand. It's the "mark of the beast" (antichrist). Don't live in fear of what is happening down there. It's gonna get real ugly-- but don't concern yourself with those things which you cannot stop or control. It is only temporary. Prepare yourself for the soon return of Jesus. He's about to split the sky wide open to call His children home! I'll be here waiting for you. See ya' soon, Thomas!

Yours For All Eternity,

William A. Taylor

About the Author

Thomas attended Baptist Bible College in Springfield, Missouri. He completed his degree in Biblical Studies at Liberty University in Lynchburg, Virginia. He has been involved in many facets of ministry including local churches, Christian schools, youth camps, and Public Relations for a major nationwide Christian television and theme park.

Now retired, Tom and his wife Liz spend their days writing and ministering the good news of deliverance.

Other Books by

Thomas A. Moore

Falwell and Bakker: The Journeys, The Scandals, The Redemption

Satan's Greatest Weapon, The Deception of Religion

Satan's Greatest Weapon, Part 2: The Deception of Idolatry

Satan's Greatest Weapon, Part 3: The Deception of Ignorance

Broken, Fallen and Rejected: God's Dysfunctional Family

Hear Me

Hide Me

Fifty Shades of Black

REFERENCES

The Conspirator's Hierarchy: The Committee of Three Hundred, (Dr. John Coleman) American West Publishers & Distributors

The New World Order, (Pat Robertson) Word Books

The Dark Secrets of the Illuminati: The Truth Revealed, (Sue Ellen) We Can't Be Beat LLC

Like Lambs to the Slaughter, (Johanna Michaelsen) Harvest House

The Secret Teachings of the Masonic Lodge, (John Ankerberg and John Weldon) Moody Publishers

None Dare Call It Conspiracy, Gary Allen Buccaneer Books

Made in the USA
Middletown, DE
26 April 2019